Problems of Participation

Problems of Participation

Reflections on Authority, Democracy, and the Struggle for Common Life

Edited by Tehseen Noorani, Claire Blencowe & Julian Brigstocke

Contributors: Claire Blencowe
Patrick Bresnihan
Julian Brigstocke
Leila Dawney
Sam Kirwan
Naomi Millner
Helen Nicholson
Tehseen Noorani
Jenny Pearce
Michel Pimbert
Tom Wakeford

ARN Press
www.authorityresearch.net

ARN Press
3 Buckwell Court, Lewes, BN7 2UE, United Kingdom.

www.authorityresearch.net
email: contact@authorityresearch.net

For distribution details, please refer to our website.

ISBN: 9780957588202

British Library Cataloguing in Publication Data

A catalogue record for this book is available from the British Library.

Contents

Detailed Contents

Preface

This book gathers together a collection of essays organized around three 'problems' of participatory democracy. These problems raise questions, conundrums and challenges for participatory practice and thinking. They point towards both difficulties and opportunities. We are not identifying 'problems' in order to simply criticize or reject participation. Problems are an enduring part of all worthwhile practice, driving creativity, understanding and skills. Our aim is to vitalize participatory thought and practice by raising and reflecting upon three broad problems.

The first problem that the essays address is that 'Participatory Democracy Needs Authority'. The authors of essays in this section affirm the value of democracy, paying particular attention to how it needs to be cultivated through structures of authority. Those who have authority and those who grant it are connected by bonds of trust that allow us to hold people and actions to account. Democracy's dependence upon authority constitutes a problem, creating challenges and dilemmas, because trust takes time and emotional labour to build and often seems to be a scarce resource. Moreover, we have to deal with the fact that there are always power relations and inequalities at play – however participatory our practice or democratic our intentions.

The second problem that we take up is that 'Participatory Democracy is a Craft'. Rather than understanding democracy in terms of electoral politics, and participation in terms of handbooks and manuals brimming with the latest techniques and models, the contributors attend to the subtleties of effective participation, whether in civil society activity, processes of collaborative learning or in 'ordinary' life. Enhancing democracy through better forms of participation requires particular ethical and embodied sensibilities and commitments, which can only be developed through practical experience, and which need to be nurtured through slow apprenticeship. Democracy is craftwork more than it is a set of institutions, textbook techniques or processes. However, as the authors of this section suggest, it is a difficult, costly and embodied *challenge* to learn the skills and ethos of such craft.

The final problem is that 'Participatory Democracy is a Struggle Against Privatization'. Many advocates of participatory democracy are more or less explicitly committed to resisting 'privatization' both in the sense of commodification and market dominance, and in the sense of individualisation of life and experience – seeing both as opposed to equality and dignity. But many proponents of neoliberal marketization and individualised freedom also promote myriad forms of 'participation'. Further, as is evident in theatre box offices, 'participation sells'. This raises awkward questions and uncomfortable challenges for proponents of participation – a challenge that the authors of this section try to address, in part, by reframing participation in terms of acting in, and creating, alternative visions of what we share in common.

We hope that this collection of essays helps in opening up conversations around participation. Such conversation is crucial, not simply for specialist communities of practitioners or academics, but for *everyone* who is interested in democracy and dignity today. 'Participation' has become nigh on ubiquitous as an ambition, description and buzzword throughout social life, from marketing strategies and economic development, through government reform and alternative politics, to education and the arts. We might even say that participation is *the* form, the mode of organisation, that defines our present moment. Participation is our condition, our imperative and our problem.

Problem One

Participatory Democracy Needs Authority

Democracy and the Reinvention of Authority

Julian Brigstocke

Over the last two hundred years, democracy has emerged as the dominant platform for authentic political participation. Even dictatorships, tyrannies and oligarchies mobilize the rhetoric of democracy to legitimize their rule. The only *true* political life, we could perhaps say, has become democratic life: for in a democratically elected government, the will of the people receives its most truthful expression.

But if true political life is democratic life, then 'truth' seems now to have been distorted out of all recognition. War, poverty, exploitation and injustice are defended in the name of the democratic will of sovereign nations. Elected representatives appear constantly on television and the radio, in order to say precisely – nothing. To tell a lie is dangerous;

but to speak truthfully is impossible because it might deviate from the official party line, undermining its credibility and authority. Safer, then, to master the art of speaking whilst saying nothing – the art of speaking in slogans. The risks of speaking the truth, with all of the nuances and subtleties that this implies, are too great. Nothing is really said; nothing really changes.

For early thinkers of modern democracy, the democratic assertion of the 'will of the people' meant voicing a collective refusal to acquiesce to poverty, exploitation and injustice. It meant denouncing the absurdity of aristocrats' claim to embody the values, virtues and soul of the nation. Democracy was to be a device for lending authority to disruptive, polemical truths about exploitation and injustice. Democracy would be a means of collectively speaking truth to power.

Democracy has always had a difficult relationship with truth. Indeed, both voters and those who represent them have often been charged with being *incapable* of truth. First to stand accused are the people themselves. The oldest criticism of democracy, dating to antiquity, was that the people are simply too ignorant to govern themselves. Power requires wisdom, and wisdom requires the knowledge that comes with education, privilege and good taste.

The boldest response to this would have been to assert unequivocally that *everyone* has an equal capacity to determine their own interests, values and aspirations. Everyone has a capacity to speak the truth. But this was not the path taken by the founders of modern democratic theory.

Instead, they asserted that the masses must be taught their true interests. Only when they are knowledgeable enough, the theory went, will they be capable of ruling wisely. The people must be educated; they must be given the wisdom to rule. This meant that the price of increased popular *power* was to be an ever tighter submission to *authority*: the capacity of teachers, professors, scientists and economists to define the nature of the world, its problems, and the possible solutions to those problems. The path was paved for the technocratic forms of democracy with which we are now all too familiar, where the field of possible solutions to social and political problems is narrowed to the point of emptiness by 'experts' in diverse fields such as economy, finance, diplomacy, and communications.

Second to stand accused of living falsely are the people we elect to act on our behalf. Political representatives are what the philosopher Thomas Hobbes described as 'artificial persons'. They are 'artificial' in the sense that they do not 'own' the words they speak. Elected politicians' words belong to those who elected them, not to themselves. They only have authority to speak in the public realm insofar as their speech represents the interests and voices of their constituents. They cannot speak truly when they speak for themselves, only when they speak in place of others.

However, there is inevitably and necessarily a gap between voters and politicians. This means that representatives can always be accused of speaking falsely. Multiple, conflicting voices and standpoints cannot be articulated by one voice, or even one political party. Hence our obsession with politicians' lies and hypocrisies, a preoccupation as old as democracy itself. Politicians are not simply deceitful because they are corrupt; they are deceitful because of the very office that they hold. For them, speaking truthfully – that is, accurately representing the will of their constituents – is simply impossible.

What these accusations amount to is a powerful and important challenge to the present structures of democratic authority. Voters are increasingly suspicious of claims to be articulating genuine truths about the world, whether these claims are made by politicians, journalists, scientists or sociologists. Increasingly, dissenters are starting to insist that *different* truths be told – truths that speak to their deeply felt experiences of injustice and marginalization.

This process is already underway. The impoverished nature of representative democracy in the 21st century is motivating a dazzling variety of experiments with new forms of democratic engagement. From participatory budgeting to citizens' juries, new forms of democratic practice are being invented that offer vastly increased power to people to transform their own lives.

However, it is vital that these new pioneers of democracy do not make the same mistake as was made in the nineteenth century. This is the mistake of putting all their energies into the democratization of power, and failing to address the democratization of authority that needs to accompany it. Democratization is not just a question of transferring more power to the marginalized (though this is essential); it is also a question of inventing new ways of speaking *truth to* power.

This means democratizing those positions that do *not* wield direct power. Democratizing authority means multiplying its sources, contesting the centralization of authority, allowing marginalized truth-claims to achieve greater visibility and purchase.

Increasing participation in the production of knowledge, ideas and capacities is a crucial way in which disruptive truths can acquire greater authority. This can be seen, for example, in the ways in which the results of certain citizens' juries have been widely reported in the media and used to hold governments to account (see for example, Tom Wakeford and Michel Pimbert's contribution to this volume). It is important, however, to understand where the authority here comes from. In citizens' juries, authority is *dramatized,* staged through performances that are designed to give the greatest possible visibility to marginalized claims and positions. New forms of participation do not give access to more 'authentic' forms of participation; but they do lend authority to new and creative forms of knowledge creation and claims making.

Democratic truth is not a state of total transparency, consensus or rational agreement. Nor is it a banal aggregation of preferences. Rather, democracy demands the creation of new voices and new provocations. These voices will not have the strength and self-assurance of the traditional bearers of authority. They will not have been 'authorized' by powerful institutions, businesses or markets. Democratizing authority requires inventing ways of amplifying hidden, whispered truths, truths that testify to experiences that have until now been silenced. In order to become authoritative, these truths must travel beyond individual experiences and find a point of contact, a lever that enables them to touch other people and other interests through their experiential intensity and resonance. What is required, perhaps, is a heightened attentiveness to the *poetics* of democracy: to the ways in which new truths are born, die away, or reignite.

The End of Authority

Jenny Pearce

Introduction: Authority and Authenticity in the Age of Horizontality

Authority has gained a bad press amongst those frustrated with the world as it is. From 1968 onwards, movements for change have often styled themselves as being 'anti-authority'. 1968 heralded what many conservatives mourn as an end of deference to authority, whether it be parental, religious, monarchical, political or cultural. However, the late twentieth century also witnessed a search, even a yearning, for authenticity: something so trustworthy and genuine, it acts as a mooring in a fast moving world of marketing and messaging which nevertheless ignites creativity. Something, in other words, to believe in and act from, without recreating the inflexibilities of truth and tradition.

Does participation, by proposing the right of everyone to take part, end authority as we know it? Or does it spur us to revisit the end(s) of authority and attune it to a 'horizontal' ethos which nevertheless must address the multiplication of differences and disagreements that accompanies increased participation?

The political philosopher Hannah Arendt began her exploration of the concept of authority in the late 1950s, with the suggestion that the confusion surrounding it derives from the fact that we can 'no longer fall back upon authentic and undisputable experiences common to all'.[1] Does authenticity become even more elusive in a participatory milieu? Does it further loosen a tether which enables people to withstand the buffers of external pressure while slackening before the winds of change?

I will argue that new forms of authority can be built through participation. Authority generated through participation is built around integrity and trustworthiness, commitment and critique. It provides stability without rigidity and strengthens capacity to discriminate between the quality of choices. Authority emerges through recognition of good judgement, a vital component for persuading others of the merits and value of participation.

We cannot, in a participation-oriented society, do away with authority. However, it must be created in totally new conditions to the past, when, as Richard Sennett argued, the recognition of authority reflected instinctive needs as much as sound orientation: 'What people are willing to believe is not simply a matter of the credibility or legitimacy of the ideas, rules, and persons offered them. It is also a matter of their own need to believe. What they want from an authority is as important as what the authority has to offer.'[2] Over time, participatory experience might gradually diminish and/or transform this 'need to believe'. In the meantime, authority continues to matter, but not the form of authority which has tended to suppress critical voice and conserve traditional relations and exercise of power. It is hard to see how preserving the order of things could underpin a society geared to widening participation in naming problems alongside building the qualities to participate in finding solutions.

Such a society will only flourish through the growth of a form of power commensurate with working together and comfortable with conflict, rather than through relations of domination and subordination aimed at containing conflict and preserving hierarchy. Such a form of power still requires authority, trusted references which survive the moment and guide action without assuming infallibility, immutability or unquestioned obedience. Hence critical capacity as well as commitment to the tasks at hand, is a foundation for claims to authority. The discussion that follows will highlight therefore the distinction between power and authority, and how power which privileges cooperation rather than domination might generate new forms of authority commensurable to a society that must work together. It suggests that the end of authority is to satisfy the human desire for trustworthy signposts and distinguishing markers, so that the 'human capacity for building, preserving, and caring for a world that can survive us' may thrive despite the 'loss of worldly permanence and reliability'.[3]

Authority and Power

Authority has been usefully contrasted with power, but mostly only with one form of power, power *over* or dominating power. The 'growing' of an alternative form of power, which could be termed 'non dominating' power, widens and deepens the potentiality for greater participation. It stimulates human cooperation and capacity to address complex challenges and conflicts. When authority is paired with non dominating power, it takes on an extra significance to the time-honoured form of authority. Arendt saw the latter as deriving (unlike power) from a foundation in the past which it augments in the lives of the living (a reference to the etymology of 'authority' in the Latin, *auctoritas from* the verb *augere,* to augment). It implies 'obedience in which men retain their freedom'. It exists prior to command and requires no external coercion. Those in authority do not have power, in fact, and Arendt quotes Cicero's famous dictum that 'while power resides in the people, authority rests with the Senate', to illustrate the distinction between power and authority as understood in Ancient Rome, in which the elders advised (in ways it was better not to ignore) but did not command.

Arendt herself has little problem differentiating authority from power, because her understanding of power is - controversially - based on an idea that power derives its legitimacy from an original collective act of consensus.[4]

Authority, vested in a person, or offices or hierarchical offices is a form of institutionalised power essential to the functioning of societies because it is instantly recognised and unquestioned and does not need to be exercised. She is much criticised, however, for her 'revisionary' redefinition of power as traditionally understood, thus obscuring the role of dominating power *over* people. She has also been criticised, more unfairly I would suggest, for eliminating conflict from the world of politics. Her foundational act of consensus does not in fact preclude subsequent conflicts over goals and actions.[5] However, she does seem to preclude the possibility of legitimate coercive power.

Indeed, non-dominating power is still often dismissed as a normative ideal. However, it is an ideal which contemporary participants in global social justice movements, for example, have begun to experiment with. Non-hierarchical movements, consensus decision making and egalitarian approaches to listening and talking have emerged over the last decade. And at the community level, many activists reject the power that dominates and excludes. In a series of conversations about power with such activists, they spoke of power as 'enabling, sharing and cooperating'.[6]

Arguably, the problem today is less about the possibilities that such a form of power might grow, and more about the making, breaking and remaking of the meanings of authority. Authority, said the activists in the power conversations, is earned through behaviour towards others which they in turn recognise as enabling of them. Trustworthy arbiters and guides emerge in this way, not from foundational myths of the past or embedded structures, or the perpetuation of child-parent relationships in the public realm. However, such authority lacks codification and suffers from the lack of respect for experiential rather than formally accredited knowledge. This limits effectiveness to act and make change in the wider world, as these community activists generally prefer to remain in their own world of power and authority.

Non-dominating power can foster participation but not necessarily in ways which generate sustainable movements for change in articulation with others. Participation needs to expand and extend the domains of human cooperation and coactive power and win the trust of others. Co-producing authority through participation advances confidence in its approach to human endeavour. Non-dominating power could itself gain authority as coercive power is reduced and its limiting effects on meaningful participation exposed. Thus, without participation, there is no impetus toward authority remaking. Without authority, participation remains the hobby of the enthusiast.

Conclusion: Participation and the Remaking of Authority

Participation appears to require its own authoritative frameworks, but what might they look like and how do they gain authority? Claire Blencowe argues that there is something fundamentally collaborative about authority, a symbiotic relationship between the dominant and the subordinate in the acceptance of authority and the reciprocity expected from it.[7] This gives authority both its illusion and potency. At the same time, authoritative relationships derive from inequalities of knowledge and some collective acceptance of some criteria of knowing. Her suggestion that *objectivity* is a key condition of authority raises the question of how participation might remake authority of a new kind through relationships which do not depend on domination and subordination or the top down privileging of certain forms of knowledge and knowing and the containment and suppression of others. Mechanisms are still needed which distinguish qualities of knowledge and relevance to problem solving.

If 'objectivity is not truth, it is the condition of living, experiencing and acting in common', then it is consistent with the logic of non-dominating or coactive power *with* as the breakthrough required for chains of command to be converted into co-deliberated and co-determined horizontalism. Such power also grows out of conflictive encounters with the desires of others, however counterposed to one's own. Mary Parker Follett saw such interactions as continuously creating a new 'whole' out of the parts and new forms of agency and community. Authority could retain its task of augmentation of such processes. However, this would not be by virtue of past and present predictability and ancient wisdom, but through the nature of the social encounter which has created it. The validation of outcomes in terms of shared and agreed criteria of quality, universality and inclusivity, recognisable to wider and wider circles of participants creates new collective meanings and trustworthy reference points. While not permanent or infallible, they are beyond the subjective. Their authority is earned. They not only do not require a foundational myth but nor do they reproduce one, only trusted, co-created moorings and navigational aids for venturing out in voyages of discovery and new learning. The exteriority of objectivity, the gap which gives it its potency beyond a mere aggregation of participant subjectivities, prevails as long as necessary to the lived experience of the activated agents of participation. Participants come to welcome their new-found responsibility in co-producing authority rather than relinquishing it in exchange for an illusory security. Remaking authority thus serves the logic of participation and the logic of participation continuously remakes the authority which serves it.

---

[1] Arendt, H. (1959) 'What is Authority?' in Baehr, P. *The Portable Hannah Arendt*, Harmondsworth: Penguin, pp. 462-507.
[2] Sennett, R. (1980) *Authority*, London: Faber and Faber, p. 25.
[3] Arendt, 'What is Authority?', p. 463.
[4] Arendt, H. (1969) *On Violence*. Harmondsworth: Penguin.
[5] Haugaard, M. (2003) 'Reflections on Seven Ways of Creating Power', *European Journal of Social Theory*, 6 (1): 87-113
[6] Pearce, J. (2012) *Power in Community: A Research and Social Action Scoping Review*
[7] Blencowe, C. (2013) 'Biopolitical Authority, Objectivity and the Groundwork of Modern Citizenship' *The Journal of Political Power.* 6 (1): 9-28

Involving Others

From Toolkit to Ethos for a Different Kind of Democracy

Naomi Millner

Here's the scenario: you are a group of individuals, concerned with the housing issues in your area. You are aware of dozens of empty buildings in various states of disrepair, whose only prospects are eventual redevelopment by private firms. Together with a group of activist friends, you begin to imagine how acquiring one of these buildings might form a hub of autonomous organising in the area. One of these derelict buildings might be the basis for a community centre with a difference, a centre of collaborative learning, a space for people of different walks of life to encounter each other. The problem is, you don't know if that's what the other people in the area would want. There's no history of autonomous organising there. Local residents you have spoken to are interested, but haven't really thought about the idea before. Some are positively against the idea, fearing that it will bring

Wall drawing on a building in Barcelona, Spain. Creative commons license.

'black-clad anarchists', graffiti vandalism, and increased crime to the area. How can you begin a process that involves more than just those in your social group? How can you ensure the process which takes place properly attends to the opinions and desires of others invested in the area, without losing sight of your vision?

Countless models, techniques and 'kits' have been created to enable decisions to be made more collaboratively. The aim of these resources is ostensibly to introduce democratic openness into a situation which risks sidelining dissident voices or alternative interests. For example, a group of scientists might use a 'participatory' approach to come up with a solution to the repeated flooding of an area that draws on the personal experience and knowledge of local people. Rather than presuming that scientific studies will give rise to the best solution, this approach acknowledges that there are many aspects of the problem which will be hidden without a more diverse array of knowledge-producers.[1] In another example, the Joseph Rowntree Foundation is interested in funding initiatives which use participative approaches to develop poverty reduction schemes. The idea here is to allow the experience and insights of people who have experienced poverty to drive the formation of solutions, as opposed to theories conceived at a remove from the actual realities of poverty.[2]

But in each scenario there is a problem to be faced. Whoever initiates the process has an interest in the question, place, or project at stake. Those invited to take part may have no interest, or a very different interest in the same object. To involve others in such a process whilst also maintaining integrity to this dissonance, something more than a set of techniques is required. A set of techniques can only lay out a recommended set of steps for action. It can't ensure attention to minority voices, or guarantee that an equitable process will take place. For these reasons, participatory approaches have been extremely susceptible to incorporation into corporate and commerce-oriented agendas. The idea of participation is an attempt to respond to the 'democratic deficit' in the contemporary western world – a lack of opportunities for everyday individuals to be substantively involved in decision-making or social change. However, the language of participation can be used without any commitment to equality. It is possible to 'consult' a local population before a large-scale property development, and to tick all the ethical boxes, whilst keeping the planned design working firmly in the interests and pockets of the developers.

So how can we take back a language of participation? Beyond a tool-kit, participation requires an *ethos* if it is to play a part in equitable social transformations. An ethos is a set of values which are embodied into repeated practice. Rather than reducing a participative process to a model which can be reproduced with lip-service, the ethos asks certain commitments and dispositions from facilitators, and involves them in a wider project for which the name is 'democracy.'

Democracy in this sense is not the same thing as the political system which, in the UK, means that we vote to have someone to represent us in the House of Commons. Instead, it is a body

Stencil art in Madison, Wisconsin. Creative commons license.

of political values which have developed through a long history to try and give rise to more just and equitable ways of organising social life. For example, anarchist and environmental social groups have devised a repertoire of 'radical democratic' practices which address less visible hierarchies of speech and listening, such as 'consensus decision-making' and co-operative financial structures.[3] Such techniques address the way that, in contemporary society, knowledge too is produced through processes which recognise the capacities of some over others. Knowledge is often produced in a manner which reproduces and sustains existing power imbalances – whether across a given society, or within a particular social movement. For example, on issues of sustainable agriculture today, scientific evidence is increasingly trusted and brought into the domain of international policy-making. But the experiential knowledge of peasant-farmers around the world, who have farmed sustainably for centuries, is rarely recognised.

The development of participatory methods marks an effort to respond to this imbalance of access to resources and a recognition of unacknowledged capacities. Yet close examination of such techniques reveals that participation today is being adopted into policy-making and planning in ways which further disempower those with a stake or interest in a particular problem. Once it has been reported that members of a local community have been 'consulted', plans for an urban generation scheme may be placed on a fast-track, and even given a 'green' status. As an ethos, a participation agenda asks for more: it entails a set of commitments which make the interests of invested parties vulnerable and open to change. By making clearer the values which are in question, the ethos also makes the participation agenda more robust and resilient against commercial co-optation.

An Ethos of Trust

Democracy in the making of knowledge or of decisions is a key aspiration for 'participative' methodologies. This means allowing all those with a stake in a problem or question to speak back to the process from its beginning to its end. But how can others be invited into a process in a manner which moves beyond the superficial? Take the case outlined in Part One. Your group *wants* to involve others. But do they want to participate? Do they know they want to participate? It can be difficult to convince people to take part. Once a group or process has been established it can be even more difficult to simultaneously pursue a goal (for example, to create an architectural plan for a disused building) and make space for participants to disagree, or introduce their own ideas. Part of an ethos for participation entails an act of giving *trust.* Only when the facilitator of a participative process actively trusts the current knowledge and abilities of those taking part can a solution be created which is able to successfully invite participants into a process, and move beyond the framing or interests of a narrow group of people.

There is a story which shows the meaning of this act of giving trust. The story is told by the political thinker Jacques Rancière in his book *The Ignorant Schoolmaster.*[4] Here Rancière follows the lesson learnt by the historical educator Joseph Jacotot (1770-1840). Jacotot was a distinguished academic, popular with his students whose 'long and eventful career should have made him immune from surprises. He was once a passionate subscriber to this technique of 'explication' for teaching – of progressing students from more simple to more complex contexts. However, he is by chance converted to new methods when, in exile in Belgium, he is approached by a number of Flemish-speaking students, who beg him to teach them as well.

Speaking only French, Jacotot cannot invite them to his classes – but he acquires for each person a bilingual edition of Fénelon's *Telemaque*, recently published in Brussels. Through a translator, he instructs the students to learn this text for themselves, repeating it over and over. Without much confidence in the experiment, Jacotot is nevertheless sufficiently astonished by the results for him to abandon a canon of methods he has preserved for decades. When he asks the students to write down their thoughts on their readings, the students not only proficiently articulate themselves in French, but express their thoughts on the first half of the book with astounding coherency. Jacotot grasps at once that despite his firmly held convictions, the students are capable of learning quite independently of *his* intelligence. From this moment he abandons the ivory towers, and goes amongst the country's poor, conducting a series of further experiments to discover how he can actualise his new discovery in such a way that all may realise what lies already within their power. This is the lesson that anyone can teach. It consists only in an act of legitimising the learning which is already taking place, outside the language of the academy. This discovery, he realises, does not need to be explicated; 'it sufficed only to *announce* it'.

The point of the 'pedagogy' – the art of teaching and learning – that Rancière draws out is that intelligence lies everywhere. To involve this intelligence in a properly democratic way is to understand it on a plane of equality. To involve this intelligence in a properly effective, 'participative' way is to learn how to make explicit our own interests in the specific problem at stake. Rather than presume the interests of others

Engraving of Joseph Jacotot (1770-1840).

we need to recognise the presence of diverse interests and forms of knowledge. A process which moves beyond a liberal, woolly lip-service to participation is thus a process of *facilitation,* where the problem identified forms a beginning point, an opening, but the solution is to be created through a reiterative return to redefining the problem. What does this mean for the vision which first inspired the process – must it be entirely surrendered? The key is to frame the problem in the initial stages in such a way that it resonates with the existing concerns of others. This requires a period of research on the part of the initiating group – conversations, encounters, and the creation of an interested 'public' in a particular object, whether this be a physical space, a barrier to collective life, a neighbourhood. The object must be larger than the problem identified, so that a diverse audience can be brought together from the perspectives of their own interests and investments. However there is still a place for leadership, and for a 'holding' of the problem, in this process. The goal of leadership is to create a structured space-time of engagement from which a journey of inquiry can emerge as a response to the initial problem. This requires a commitment on the part of the facilitators to suspend their own hopes, views, and intelligence with regard any possible solution, whilst continuing to exert their 'will' in fidelity to their initial inspiration to act. Jacotot didn't give up on his role as a 'pedagogue' – someone wilfully engaged in a process of shared teaching and learning. But through his experiments he learnt that he must refrain from relying upon his own intelligence to convince his participants of the nature of the problem, and invite them instead to play their part in defining it. This commitment brings values of trust, listening and openness to the centre of an ethos for participation.

Trust, Listening and Openness

Trust is not only a matter of realising and legitimising the capacities of others. It also means establishing a 'space of trust' in which participants feel their involvement is structured and their contributions are respected. Establishing spaces of trust mean that individuals can feel confident to speak out in ways they are not used to, or take risks which make them feel vulnerable.

I have another story to show what this looks like in practice. It is drawn from my research with young people in Bath and Bristol who were not in education or training. They were enrolled in 'access' courses to get back into education, and I was working with a research project that was testing and developing models for enhancing individuals' capacities to learn. I worked with a group of teenagers who had left school without gaining any qualifications. My task was to adapt an inquiry-based learning process, designed by researchers for other groups, to enable these individuals to become aware of their own existing interests and knowledge, and the connections between these interests and existing fields of knowledge. In the process, each individual identified a place or object which fascinated them. One person chose Cheddar Gorge, the last place she remembered being truly happy with her family, before her parents split up. Another chose a picture of himself visiting a famous racing car demo, and sitting in a red Ferrari, since this had inspired his interest in racing. A third chose the quarry she had visited for free parties at which she felt most herself. Each person then created a project book in which the object was documented, measured, revisited, and studied. After this, I worked with them to draw out and write down key questions which had arisen during the documentation process: how was Cheddar Gorge formed? Had anyone ever lived there? What do we know about its past?

In individual supervisions we linked these questions with areas of existing study, and each person was supported to develop the skills to find out their own answers, and share them with the group.

The project surprised me with its successes. One boy chose 'the Sun' as his object and ended up making a connection with a local astronomer to view the Sun through an optical telescope. Although the boy was profoundly dyslexic, he created a Powerpoint presentation for the group introducing them to the physical and astrophysical specificities of the Sun, and involving them in his questions about its chemical composition. But when I asked the group about why and how they had each produced such brilliant work, opening new intellectual avenues for themselves, they surprised me again. It wasn't so much the methodology, they said, as the personal trust that had been developed through individual meetings that had encouraged them to take the risks with their involvement, and the small steps we had taken along the way. Feeling heard and feeling safe made them feel able to go along with the process, although most confessed they hadn't really seen the point of it until they were quite a long way in. The quality of relationships and the trust invested in them was more important than the techniques for participation.

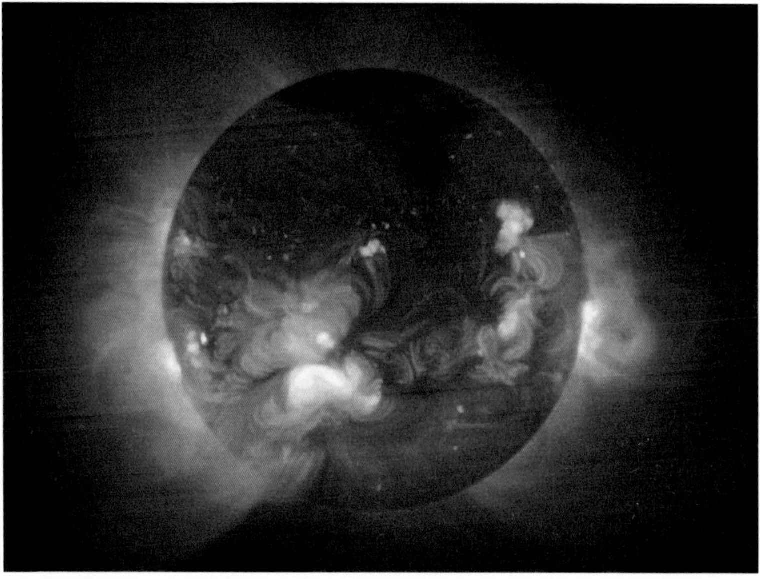

The Sun as viewed by the Soft X-Ray Telescope (SXT) onboard the orbiting Yohkoh satellite.

Trust in others and spaces of trust are best established when the participative process is seen as one of *inquiry*. There is a problem at stake identified by the facilitator, and others are 'co-investigators'. To bring of their knowledge and experience to the inquiry, sufficient intermediate steps must be made for links to be made between participants' own invested interests, and those of the facilitator. The facilitator acts as a 'learning guide' or pedagogue during the inquiry, and structures the intermediate steps. However he or she does not have the final framing of the problem – that belongs to the group. This calls for a reiterative process in which the facilitator actively listens to what is emerging from the exercises, and allows it to build into a collective sense of momentum. Active listening in this sense means attending to the responses – visceral, linguistic, and tentative – of the group to draw out emergent directions. From this point the facilitator will be in a position to rearticulate the problem and remaining parts of the inquiry process, in a way resonant with this momentum, and to make it explicit and accessible to participants. This requires a difficult level of openness to disagreements, new tensions, and unforeseen directions. However it will result in an affective, felt sense of ownership within a given group, and will allow for the development of a solution which far exceeds the imagination and experience of the facilitator(s).

Authority as the Capacity to Inspire Trust

What is the place of 'authority' within the collaborative relationship between the facilitator of a participative process, and participants? Authority, then, is not about coercive power or a manipulation of others for personal interests. Authority is *granted* to a teacher, government official, or leader, when others recognise and value the tradition or experience which set that individual apart. The facilitator of a participative process has authority when those involved invest them with a certain distance, or 'outside' status. Science has authority in an investigation when it is accorded the weightiness to govern and influence decisions. But within an 'ethos' of participation there is another layer to add to authority. *Authority is a capacity to inspire trust.* This is what marks a participative inquiry apart from the liberal models which consult others, but never fully recognise, nor invite, their intelligence. By structuring an inquiry in such a way as to involve others and their experience in the making of knowledge, and by drawing these forms of knowledge onto an externally recognised platform of validation (eg. scientific practice), a facilitator is creating something which can be relied upon. This something reflects the interests of those whom the problem at stake concerns *and* it can be compared and translated into the languages of science and policy-making. In this sense an ethos of participation can take part in the making of democratic forms of knowledge, which can be trusted for guiding new ways of governing and organising social life. Beyond tokenistic representation this is a matter of remaking the social through authoritative, trust-full relationships.

---

[1] See, for example, Whatmore, S. J. & Landström, C. (2011) 'Flood Apprentices: An Exercise in Making Things Public', *Economy and Society*, 40(4), 582 - 610.

[2] See Bennett, F. & Roberts, M. (2004) *Participatory Approaches to Research on Poverty*, Joseph Rowntree Foundation). Available at: http://www.jrf.org.uk/publications/participatory-approaches-research-poverty.

[3] See http://www.seedsforchange.org.uk/

[4] Rancière, J. (1991) *The Ignorant Schoolmaster*, Stanford: Stanford University Press.

Participatory Knowledge Matters for Democracy

Claire Blencowe

Democracy is not just about the formal structures of elections and political representation; democracy is more fundamentally about where authority rests in society. A democratic society is one where ordinary people have authority; enough authority to make political demands, to hold people to account, to be taken seriously. This is why there is an essential link between democracy and dignity. Democratisation is about the dispersal of authority throughout society. So what is 'authority' and how can participatory practices create it or redistribute it? These questions lead us to think about the ways in which different people are characterised as knowing, or not knowing, about 'reality' or 'the real world'. They even suggest that 'knowing reality' is a battleground of democracy.

What is authority?

Authority derives from people having different knowledges and experiences. We grant authority to others because we suspect that they know better than we do, or have access to some reality that is beyond us – be that access to insider knowledge or the objective facts, to the big picture or the strings of power in an institution. Authority is generally tied to particular circumstances or types of question – I'm an authority in this situation, you're an authority in that. It isn't something that we possess as individuals but rather comes from the different relationships we have to realities that lie outside of us.

In utilitarian action-orientated societies, such as those of the over-developed world today, authority is particularly bound up with the experience of having *done* something and having 'really lived'. We see people as authoritative when they have made a real contribution, (impacting on the lives of others, making something happen), when they have encountered and explored hidden 'secrets of life', or when they have gone through some transformative life experience. This happens in all sorts of different ways. Most obviously we grant authority to various 'experts': people who, through scientific training or experience, know a great deal about some specific and important area of life. But we also grant authority to people who have gone through particularly intense 'real life' experiences of injustice or suffering; or who go beyond their own interests, to work for other people, caring for or creating life and capacities.

Participation in the institutions and practices of scientific expertise is a really important source of authority. Scientists have a kind of privileged access to 'reality', using special techniques and technologies to observe causes and forces that are invisible to the ordinary eye. Scientists have a specialised knowledge that makes them closer to the 'objective' or 'hard' facts, and they can often draw authority from that relative proximity. Medical science and practice is perhaps the greatest source of authority in this respect because it is both a set of knowledges about hidden realities and a set of practices for intervening in and caring for the health of other people. Medical doctors participate in innovative science and technological advance, achieving great things in knowledge, but also sacrificing themselves for others, providing care, and touching on the very limits of life – facing death and illness, or bringing new life into the world. This makes for some highly authoritative figures.

Our societies also grant a great deal of authority to people that have participated in the 'real world' of markets, financial risk and wealth creation. Entrepreneurs, economists and ratings agencies sit amongst the most authoritative figures in our societies – those whose opinions are seen to matter, who issue advice that can't safely be ignored. Such figures have participated in the domain of life that is (often portrayed as) most *fully real*; they have contributed to economic life, taken risks, encountered 'the bottom line'. Market-experience based authority seems to become ever more significant. In the UK, for example, scientists and doctors themselves increasingly have to engage in market practices – being called upon to justify their authority by stepping down from the ivory towers to participate in the 'real world' of market competition. The authority of entrepreneurs, financiers and economists isn't just about these people being wealthy and having financial clout. In part their authority comes from the sense that they have engaged with, been close to, experienced the 'real world' of economic necessity and market forces. Indeed, recent events in banking demonstrate that such figures do not even have to have been successful or acted legitimately in order to be authoritative – perhaps because whatever their role they have nonetheless been very *close to* this all important reality. In the fall-out of the financial crisis experts on financial matters became all the *more* likely to have their voices listened to in public debate, despite such experts having been in significant respects responsible for the crisis. We could say that the figures of finance claimed an authority relative to the crisis precisely *because* they had participated in its creation.

These forms of authority (scientific expertise and market-experience based authority) are exclusionary, elitist and so anti-democratic. The authority of scientific expertise and medicine is obviously intertwined with inequalities of access to education, technology and time. It takes an awful lot for someone to become a participant in advanced scientific experiments. It is easier to participate in market forces than it is to participate in the developments of bio-chemistry; but market-experience based authority has some really anti-democratic implications of its own. Market-experience based authority can radically compound marginalisation by characterising the economically excluded in infantilising terms, as people who 'lack experience', who have not 'made a contribution', or have not 'really lived'. Such characterisations make it all too easy for elites to ignore the views of ordinary people. In the recent rhetoric of the UK government, the supposed 'shirkers' (the un- or under-employed and those unable to work) are said to keep the blinds on their windows drawn – a caricature that paints these people as themselves *blind* to what is going on 'out there in the real world' and provides yet another excuse for politicians to ignore their voices, insights and concerns. These ways of thinking, and talking, about 'the real world' can undermine the dignity and *self*-respect of ordinary economically excluded people, such that it becomes very hard to even articulate a view or political demand in the first place... let alone to have one's view heard and respected.

Participatory practices can be technologies for redistributing authority, challenging such elitism. We can think about that challenge to elitism in at least two different ways.

Widening Participation

First: participatory processes can expand access to the kinds of experience that are normally the preserve of experts and those with the means to achieve specialist status. Procedures that involve ordinary people in decision making can effectively expand access to 'real life experience' – generating opportunities for ordinary people to act within domains of life that are thought of as really important. Participatory practice can be engines creating and redistributing authority, dignity and confidence. Widening participation in scientific analysis (especially medicine), or economic risk taking, is particularly fruitful in this respect, because of the great significance that is attached to these domains of life in our societies. To do science, or to be involved in markets and economics, is to have greater authority on public issues. In this sense, participatory practice is not simply about enabling ordinary people to 'have a say' in a particular policy decision but is potentially also about more profound and enduring changes in the distribution of authority; creating new expertise, dignity and confidence amongst participants.

Thinking about participation in this way – as attempts to disperse authority by widening participation in 'real life experience' – highlights the importance of risk and openness in participatory practice. If a participatory practice is to contribute to the dispersal of authority it cannot be tokenistic or scripted in advance (such as in those 'consultation exercises' that enable participants to choose between narrowly prescribed options through carefully managed deliberations). Participatory practices that involve ordinary people in scientific decisions (be that the approval of a drug for sale, the working out of flood defences or deciding farming strategies) should involve genuine opportunities for knowledge creation, experimental investigation and reconfiguration of the question or stakes. This is to say that such processes should be real events of scientific enquiry – not simply ways of telling people about already-established scientific facts. Likewise, participatory budgeting is meaningless from the point of view of dispersing authority unless there is a 'real' budget, substantial enough to make a proper difference to the people or problem concerned and to mean that there is a genuine financial *risk* involved. If collaborative science or participatory budgeting does not incorporate some openness to calamity and creativity, to the world pushing back, then it will not have the effect of generating 'real life' experience and redistributing authority.

Thinking about the issues in this way also points to a potential problem with the promotion of participation, from the point of view of equality and democratisation. Widening participation in a particular set of practices (such as scientific enquiry or market economics) does, in a sense, confirm the importance and authority of that practice. This, in turn, can add even more authority to the existing elites within those fields of practice and compound present inequality. For example, incorporating more people into biochemical enquiry, and holding up such science as an especially important practice in which ordinary people should be engaged, confirms to the world the significance of this mode of understanding and creates a greater investment in this way of knowing. Such a confirmation of the importance of biochemistry is not 'democratising' from the point of view of advocates of, say, holistic or behavioural approaches to medicine - who already struggle to have their voices heard relative to the bio-chemical model. A similar dynamic is at the heart of many people's concerns about the 'participatory turn' in international development work of the past two decades – where 'pro-poor' participatory practice seems to sit all too comfortably alongside neo-liberal economic strategies that can undermine the very living conditions of impoverished people. Involving 'local people' in the decisions and direction of capitalist development is inclusive and can foster dignity, but it can also be seen as a kind of 'co-option' that garners support and strength for one model of how things should be done. This is all the more problematic because the newly active 'local' participants in development practice can only ever be playing 'catch up' relative to the *already* 'expert' international development agencies. Whilst overcoming the abjection and indignity of exclusion by widening participation in various domains of reality, we can at the same time compound existing hierarchy by cementing given ideas about what is real and what matters. This seems to be an inescapable danger of widening participation.

Transforming Reality

Second, participatory practice can work to redefine what counts as 'participating in reality', by changing and challenging understandings of what 'reality' is in the first place. It is possible to redistribute authority by changing perceptions about what is important – what makes things happen – and thus changing ideas about who has participated in such happening; who has 'real life experience', which demands to be respected. Changing understandings of determination has the effect of changing what counts as 'real life experience', 'knowledge of reality', or as 'making a contribution'. We can disperse the authority that attaches to scientific expertise by changing accepted definitions of what constitutes scientific practice. Likewise, we can build up the authority and dignity of different groups of people by establishing a broader and more plural view of what constitutes economic reality.

Whilst it might seem either politically irrelevant or overly radical to attempt to change what counts as reality, this has in fact been a long standing and often successful strategy of the feminist movement. By making the personal political, for example, feminists created authority for those people (often women) who deal with the mess of personal life. A particular strategy of much feminist writing has been to transform accepted definitions of and understandings of what the economy is made of – highlighting the necessity to the 'official economy' of various domains of life that have been wrongly categorised as private matters. Feminists have long demanded recognition for domestic labour, biological reproduction and familial socialisation as 'real work', upon which everything else depends. Such arguments have impacted upon who is seen as contributing to the economy and to society at large, who has 'real life' experience, and who can claim public authority. 'Community Economy' action researchers and activists have taken up this mantel in recent years. They work to establish new visions of economic reality, wherein the 'formal economy' of capitalist relations is recognised as being no more than the 'tip of the ice-berg' of economic activity. They do projects with communities, including communities who are officially classified as 'economically inactive', to highlight the wide and varied ways in which people do actually already participate in economic reality. At the same time they work to create new community-based practices of production and exchange. These projects are not about widening participation in capitalist markets and development, but rather seek to diversify understandings of what *counts* as economic reality and so proliferate the range of activities that count as meaningful real life economic experience. These movements work for dignity and the greater dispersal of authority.

Changing accepted norms around what counts as reality is more difficult than creating new opportunities for 'widening participation'. But such change also has a more radical potential with respect to effecting democratisation. And such radical and democratising changes *have* happened in the past. The nineteenth century saw a great shift in the understanding of what reality is – with the establishment of the idea of public welfare, national security and economy alongside the new sciences of society. New objects of knowledge and practice were identified, including various processes of collective growth or decline, whilst various existing activities were reclassified as the *causes* or determinants of those processes. For example parenting transformed (in public understanding) from a private practice into a paramount *cause* of national wellbeing or decline. New forms of state and philanthropic policy were rapidly developed to impact upon this newly paramount domain. These shifts in thinking about the nature of reality had a tremendous impact upon the distribution of authority in public life in the twentieth century; contributing to the immense successes of the women's movement, the political recognition of 'labour', dramatic extensions of suffrage, and the creation of the welfare state.

Whether or not such a revolution is underway, or even possible, today (and how could we know if it were?) we should understand that debates concerning the nature of reality, knowledge and causation, are no mere 'academic exercises' – petty diversions for overly-privileged minds. Such debates are, or can be, the very battleground of democracy. Accepted theories concerning what causes things to happen, what connects things to each other, what is the basis of growth – these theories determine what counts as 'real life', who has had 'real life experience' or access to reality, and who – on the basis of such experience – can claim dignity, exercise authority, and make effective demands. Challenging and transforming such accepted ways of thinking, identifying new objects of knowledge, can constitute a major event in the making of democracy.

Problem Two

Participatory Democracy Is a Craft

Participation Stories:

The Problem of What Happens When People Don't Do What We Want Them To

Leila Dawney

Four Provocative Stories

In the UK, lorry drivers used to be paid good money. Now for an HGV1 driver, the going rate is about £8 per hour. Agency drivers who will work for less, who come from countries with weaker economies, who aren't paying rent for a family home in expensive parts of the UK, are able to offer cheaper rates for their labour. The threat of redundancy reduces drivers' powers to take action. Further pressure from government restructuring, precarious work, a failing economy, lack of affordable housing and rising fuel and food prices calls for a collective identification of a problem. This takes place in the local spaces of workplaces, pubs and homes. Threats to livelihoods are collectively articulated in terms of immigration and the protection of jobs, homes and ways of life against new competition for those resources. Organisation takes place and people are encouraged to take action. They go on an English Defence League march. There is a release of anger and frustration at the march, a collective recognition of right and wrong, of common enemies and a sense of solidarity and of mutual action that feels good. They feel like their voices get heard.

Is this participation?

Eight year old Sarah Payne is killed. Her parents campaign across the UK for 'Sarah's Law'. They have identified a problem – that there are convicted sex offenders living close to families whose parents remain unaware of, and cannot therefore act to keep their children away from. Her parents campaign for a change in the law to name and shame sex offenders in the area.

Is this participation?

A group of climate activists take over a disused school. It had been derelict for about 10 years. They put up tents and dig vegetable beds and claim the space for the people, as a community garden. They bemuse local residents by inviting them for a cup of tea. The activists smoke dope and lounge in the sun, and do not go to work. People living nearby see them as city-types and feel that the move to claim the site has come from outside the locality. They do not feel they can visit the community garden, even though they are invited by the occupiers. They continue to take their children to the public park in the middle of town. When local residents do visit the community garden, no one claims to be in charge. There is no plan for the space. One visitor asks if she can pick apples from the site, as she had done for years. They reply that of course she can, but can she share them with the people living on the site. The apples had been common before, and now it is as though there is a tax on gathering them. The attention that the protestors bring to the site means that the local council evicts the activists and erects high fences around the site, where before there were none. The activists move on to their next project, and the local residents are left with less common space than they had before.

Is this participation?

Millions of people globally protest against a war they feel is unjust, illegal and unnecessary. Their governments do not listen. The democracy organisation, *38 Degrees*, gathers over half a million signatures asking the UK government to reconsider their plans to sell off State-owned woodland. The government listens.

Is this participation?

The above examples show that in some cases, active participation in political life, in promoting change, may lead to some changes that perhaps don't have the results that we might imagine we want. Perhaps one question that we do need to start asking, then, is whether when we want to encourage participation, do we just want to encourage people to think more like 'we' do? Several essays in this book, it is argued that we should trust in others' intelligence. But what if we do and they work towards a world that we find troubling? A world of vigilantes or racists?

The Occupy movement contains some exciting ideas; it produced autonomous spaces; it has provided alternative models for politics and linked up a global movement of activism, but it has not gripped the majority of the population. To many people who are trying to get by in an increasingly neoliberalised world , politics articulated in this form does not look like the sort of thing that is commensurate with the ebbs, flows and trappings of their everyday lives. They are not in a position to take time off work, leave their families or camp in a strange city. The modes of engagement of the Occupy activists do not appeal enough to sacrifice other aspects of their lives. Indeed, activist politics is seen by many as not something 'people like us' do, and this is increasingly true since the decline of political party membership and trade union participation. The *otherness* of Occupy protestors outside St Pauls Cathedral in London from 2011-2012, and in other public spaces around the world, can make people angry. In part, this can be explained by a fear of people whose affective engagement and interest in issues is too strong. We are taught to question their motives, and ask what is lacking in their lives that makes them shout so loud. Certainly, those who devote hours of their time to their causes may get listened to, but are they the ones we *should* listen to? If not, why not? How can they speak of their misfortune, and claim to speak for us when they have had the privilege of an education; when they don't seem to work or pay any taxes?

These are the very real problems of the agenda of participation when it is articulated in an 'activist' form. Clearly participation cannot and does not always lead to a better life for all, and an embracing of participatory approaches may be damaging. Helen Nicholson's piece in this volume argues that participation in performance is becoming commodified, and Naomi Millner suggests that consultation practices may disempower more than empower. What we do know is that we need to come up with ways of analysing what participation *does,* and also what its knock-on effects are outside the space of participation itself.

The question of participation is always a question of knowledge, authority and ideology. In participatory environments, such as citizens' juries, student occupations and action research situations, participants are considered to hold expertise. This may be due to formal, institutionally-sanctioned means, such as holding a public post or qualifications. It may be due to the experiential knowledge, for example of living in a particular community, or having first-hand experiences of the issues at stake.[1] In many such spaces, participants are considered to have equal standing, and their voices to count equally. But we also need to ask how these assumptions of equal status play out in practice. How are particular knowledges and bases for expertise granted greater or lesser power? How important is language, voice, embodiment or size? What does it mean to grant equal status to someone who has been assaulted and to someone who has been researching assault for 20 years? Does this perceived equal status actually ring true during the course of the participatory exercise? Or are old habits of granting greater legitimacy to signifiers of traditional authority figures reverted to in the absence of hierarchical structures?

Where new forms of authority emerge through participatory models, what are the processes through which expertise is granted and participants are listened to? We must engage critically with new forms of participatory democracy, such as consensus decision-making – now widely used by political activists – in order to address who is listened to, and indeed which embodied capacities are mobilised in drawing listeners. Who are the 'leaders' in this process? Is consensus always a good thing? Do some speak louder and/or are some voices drowned out? When we praise participation, we want to trust other people to do the right thing, yet we might already hold certain ideas about what that is. I think that one of the problems with this line of thinking is that there is an assumption that, if everyone thought about things as much as we do, they would think the same as we do, and they would want the same things as us. And the idea that people might not, scares us. So maybe we need to be honest about this: we are interested in participation because perhaps we think that it will lead to a better world than we have at the moment. And yet we have particular and partisan ideas about what we mean by 'better'.

There are forms of participation that lead to exclusion, identitarianism and fascism, and then other forms which are inclusive, emancipatory and egalitarian. Some forms of participation that start off in the latter camp can end up coagulating into the former. If we believe that the latter is better, then that offers a normative starting point for fostering these forms and prevent them from being captured or seized by more exclusive forms.

As people who are interested in bringing about change, we do believe certain things are fundamentally wrong with the world, and we believe this because our lives have taken shape in such a way that has made us think about these things. We think that we can see things that other people do not yet have the eyes to see, and that we are in a position to help with that. Positive, inclusive modes of participation will come about when that commitment extends beyond the self and those immediately around us; when responsibility extends outwards to recognise the knock-on effects of our actions, and when we endeavour equally to develop an ethos of sensitivity to the world.

---

[1] For example, see Dawney, L. (2013) 'The Figure of Authority', *Journal of Political Power*, 6(1); Noorani, T. (2013) 'Service User Involvement, Authority and the 'Expert-by-Experience' in Mental Healthcare', *Journal of Political Power*, 6(1).

What Makes Participation Democratic?

Jenny Pearce

Participation is often associated with a normative project which historically has been about making democracy more democratic. It is inspired, like democracy itself, by 5th century Athenian politics. It pits itself against 'representative' democracy, which emerged in the eighteenth century as an alternative to the model of the Ancient Greeks. While the latter stressed that all citizens, irrespective of their socio-economic standing and assets (with the notorious exception of women, slaves and foreign-born, the 'non citizens' of that epoch) should have an equal say in the direction of state policy, 'representative democracy' was originally about restricting those who governed to those who had the attributes of wealth and education considered essential for the task. 'Representatives' would be elected by people similar to themselves. The struggle to extend the franchise to working men, women and ethnic minorities proved a long and difficult process. And although universal suffrage was eventually won in many parts of the world, those same demographics remain very unrepresented in the legislative and executive bodies of the State even in the most longstanding of representative systems.

Unlike democracy, which went onto be widely accepted as the most desirable form of political organisation, the participatory component did not. Indeed, for many, participation remained an ancient ideal no longer relevant to large-scale nations. Democracy continues to be a theoretically contested normative project, but in the early 21st century, few openly defend its alternatives. However, by the late twentieth century, a sense of 'democracy disenchantment' had emerged. Fewer and fewer people seemed motivated to use their right to vote, in the Western hemisphere at least. By contrast, in Iran some died struggling for free elections; the appeal of the right to vote resonated where the right to vote had not come to mean merely a way of registering a preference and not much more. Even in the West, however, participation on the streets seemed to grow at the same time as party affiliation and voting declined. New forms of protest arose, from the anti-globalisation movements of the 1990s to the Occupy movements of 2010. Interest in the arena of associationalism outside of the state led to the rebirth in the 1990s of the eighteenth century idea of 'civil society', which had originally accompanied the rise of markets and the new bonds forged amongst merchants and manufacturers. The post-Cold War return of liberal (neoliberal) economics revived interest in this non-state arena. Democracies, it was argued needed 'civil societies' to hold states accountable. This raised new questions about the role of organized, relative to non-organized, citizens in representative democracies.

The recognition of the non-formal spaces of public action and opinion formation coincided with the loosening of structures of authority and authorship, expertise and erudition. In the arts and architecture, in mass and social media, audiences became participants. Horizontal networks rather than top-down messaging generated new information flows, facilitated by the Internet and the smartphone. Confidence in the authoritative voice of the 'representative' over the 'represented' began to dissipate. By January 2012, the World Economic Forum in Davos acknowledged the threat of a 'dystopian future' where political and economic elites might lose the confidence of future generations. A global survey released days before the meeting showed a sharp drop in public trust in business and especially governments around the world.

These trends suggest two important themes. The first is the distinction between 'participation' and 'participatory democracy' and the second is about the qualities which make participation participative. 'Participation' I would argue is not normative. At the very least, the way in which people 'take part' in public life, is infinitely variable and varied. 'Taking part' is motivationally neutral and the dynamics behind any particular act of participation requires empirical research. The trends point not in fact to demands for participatory democracy, but rather to a self-generating process of selective involvement in new forms of shared public life and which need to be investigated to determine their significance. Why for instance, how and when, do people take part in the English Defence League (EDL)? This organisation or social movement states its aims as 'peacefully protesting against militant Islam'[1] and argues that it is defending democracy against the threat of extremist Islam. If, however, democracy is associated with political procedures to minimise conflict or at least manage it, then the EDL's confrontational style does not have democratic intent and its protests are in fact, accompanied by a threat of, if not actual, violence. Yet it is participatory. And it rests to some extent on an understanding of the polis similar to that of Athens, which delineated between citizens and non-citizens, in which the former were exclusively freeborn males of Athenian ancestry. While the EDL is not wanting to exclude all 'non-English born' from the polis, it clearly wishes to exclude those with a certain socio-religious affiliation while some of its members would go well beyond that. The challenge those of us face who wish to make arguments for participation is therefore, what makes it democratic?

The second distinction from the trends discussed above is what is really participative about participation, what are the qualities that define taking part as something active and activating of change in the status quo. Increasingly, it has been suggested, audiences have become participants. But this is often in the form of preference expression. Radio and television programmes make extensive use of such mechanisms for 'involving audiences'. Yet, such forms of participation usually influence an outcome (eg the favoured 'new star') rather than the rules of the game itself. Expert judges and professionals continue to make those decisions. Other forms of participation, however, such as Occupy, consciously organise news methods for enabling participants to actively engage in directing the movement and scrutinising its principles and their exercise, such as consensus decision making through assemblies. These kind of mechanisms experiment at least with the participative substance of participation.

Where Athens stood out is that it restricted the political privileges of its elite, though they retained their social and economic ones.[2] The extent to which the experience of democracy is curtailed by poverty and inequality has been often discussed. But, less often discussed is whether enhanced participation amongst the non-represented, the non-elites and those outside the increasingly professionalised and distant world of formal 'politics' might enable a new set of priorities and possibilities to penetrate and even transform that world? The question of what kind of knowledge and expertise for what kind of outcomes can be posed if the possibilities generated by participative process can be freed from *a priori* boundaries and expectations. Participation does become something scarily uncertain. However, this can be recognised as creative and constructive if we invest intellectual effort in understanding better the substantive dynamics and challenges that arise when people participate.

We need, therefore, to think through how to deal with the many thorny issues around participation. There are still fears of 'excessive participation'. As participatory spaces open from 'above' or from 'below', they are often complex and messy.

People bring to them varied personal experiences and predispositions. Participation in distinct spheres of public life might not imply participation in the spaces for politics and decision-making, but what is the link between the two? We need, in short, to start thinking more deeply about what might make participation democratic. Below are ten suggestions. A brief summary of the ideas behind them would emphasise the following:

Participation that is democratic is a process of enabling shifts in opinion and awareness of the interests of others which encourages better judgements to emerge around issues of public concern. It is democratic, because its component processes and procedures work towards the possibility of enhanced involvement in public affairs based on the recognition of the equal worth of all human beings. In this way individuals learn that they might fulfill their lives better through the pursuit of their own interests while always taking account of the interests of others and learning to value and deal with disagreements, conflicts and differences. In this sense, participation in increasing areas of public life, whether these be the arts or the media, the local or the national spheres, contributes towards the wider possibilities of representative democracy becoming participative in ways which in turn extend and transform its democratic potentialities.

Ten Propositions On: What Makes Participation Democratic?

EQUAL WORTH OF HUMAN BEINGS: The idea that humans are of equal worth is not the same as saying that all human beings are equal. In fact human beings are different, with varied capacities and skills. These differences are important for problem-solving. Participatory processes have to acknowledge that such differences will permeate any space of social encounter and also that they will lead to disagreements and sometimes conflicts. Disagreement and conflict are the substance of human life, to be embraced in ways that build non-violent interactions and transforming possibilities.

PARTICIPATION THAT IS DEMOCRATIC HAS NO *A PRIORI* SUBJECT: Unlike past (including Ancient Greek) understandings of who is the 'democratic subject' and who is not, participation that is democratic assumes that democratic subjectivity is constructed through participating in conditions which consciously aim to make such subjectivity possible. Thus, neither socioeconomic status nor educational level should define worthiness to participate or be grounds for exclusion.

PARTICIPATION THAT NURTURES WISDOM AND JUDGEMENT STRENGTHENS DEMOCRATIC SUBJECTIVITY: Neither wisdom nor judgement come from wealth and education and thus participation challenges the foundational assumption of representative democracy. Both wisdom and judgement are qualities which are difficult to define, but which suggest a maturity around difference and disagreement, the self in relationship to others, and recognition of the dangers of dominating forms of power. These important qualities can be strengthened through participation which simultaneously gives such qualities opportunity to demonstrate their worth.

Wisdom and judgement makes it possible to recognise valuable expertise without subjugation before it.

WIDENING WORLDVIEWS: Participatory activity is a process of enabling individuals to *widen their worldviews* through engagement with others. People come to any space of participation with limited experiences and partial knowledges. Participation exposes people to the views and knowledges of others, from whom they must be encouraged to learn as well as contributing their own. The participatory space must therefore be conducive to such mutual learning and reciprocal sharing.

TAKING ACCOUNT OF THE OTHER: The participatory activity should enable individuals to see their own *interests* in the light of those of others. Politics is all about the trade-offs involved in public decision-making over limited resources. A capacity to balance one's own needs against those of others, contributes to better politics.

PARTICIPATION THAT OFFERS INDIVIDUALS OPPORTUNITIES TO REWRITE THE SCRIPTS OF THEIR SOCIALISATION HISTORIES ENCOURAGES CHANGE AND CHALLENGE: If participation is to open up entrenched opinions, challenge assumptions and scripts which people have learnt from childhood and later socialisation experiences, it must invite people to embrace change safely. Receptivity to change and challenge-inducing participation help avoid the tendencies towards rigid bureaucratisation and hierarchisation that some suggest all democratic organisations are vulnerable to.

ACKNOWLEDGEMENT OF WHO IS NOT PRESENT: Participatory processes take care to avoid the dangers of reproducing new forms of unacknowledged or unilaterally claimed representation. It may not be possible for all those affected by a decision or an activity to be present. Questions need to be asked about who is making decisions for whom and how those absent can be made aware of the implications of decisions and given the opportunity to be involved. Delegation and representation are not intrinsically non-democratic, they just require procedures to align them with the principles of inclusion. Experiments with new methods of circulating roles should be possible, eg, sortition or lot as means for giving everyone who wants it a chance to be part of the process.

PARTICIPATION THAT IS DEMOCRATIC CREATES AUTHORITY RATHER THAN DEFERS TO PRE-EXISTING AUTHORITY: Individuals bring personal histories to the participatory space, emerging from their relationships to authority figures such as parents and teachers, leaders and celebrities. Participation that is democratic offers a new basis for authority which also challenges the child/parent or follower/leader patterns. Examples might be authority gained from recognition of contributions to the participatory encounter, such as capacity for persuasive argument, ability to address disagreement productively, and the demonstration of integrity or skills in identifying solutions to intractable problems.

PARTICIPATION GROWS MORE INCLUSIVE THROUGH NON-DOMINATING POWER: Power which is used to enable the other and build capacity to act alone as well as in concert democratises the space of encounter by making it inclusive and cooperative.[3]

LAYERED AND SCALED SPACES OF PARTICIPATION VITALISE THE POLITY: Participation does not imply that everyone has to be in the same face-to-face encounter at the same time, such as a grand participatory assembly. Plurality of levels and spaces of interaction, including virtual ones, can contribute to democratising the whole.

---

[1] Accessed at http://englishdefenceleague.org on 22 October 2012.

[2] Ober, J. (1989) *Mass and Elite in Democratic Athens: Rhetoric, Ideology, and the Power of the People*, Princeton: Princeton University Press, p.7.

[3] On 'non-dominating power', see J. Pearce (2013) 'Power and the Activist: From the Neighbourhood to the Square', *Development and Change*, 44(3).

Opening Participatory Democracy's Black Box

Facilitation as Creative Bricolage

Tom Wakeford and Michel Pimbert

Like other contributors to this book, we support participatory and action research processes as part of a diverse and growing movement to democratise processes that generate authority - in both knowledge-generation and policy-making. Like Jenny Pearce, we have found that people who are offered such opportunities welcome their new-found responsibility as holders of authoritative knowledge. Among the roles vital to any such process is that of the facilitator – a person or people who act as intermediaries in participatory processes between different holders of authority – ranging from policy-makers to everyday citizens. We have experience of being on the giving and receiving ends of a wide range of approaches to facilitation.

According to the context, facilitators may be called animateurs, convenors or mediators.

The process of facilitation is often assumed to be intellectually dull and the skills required relatively trivial. As such it has become one of the many analytic 'black boxes' in the study of participatory processes. While the interests of different authority-holders, the psychology of participants and their expertise have been exhaustively examined in academic studies and policy analyses, the process of facilitation itself has been largely ignored. By contrast the best facilitators constantly undertake such self-critical reflections in their own practice, usually in isolation from academic analysts. One exception to this is the detailed study of facilitation made by Celia Davies and her team.[1] They conclude that the quality of facilitation in deliberative democratic processes plays a crucial part in determining both inclusivity and competence.

The study of Davies *et al.* was a meticulous de-construction of a particular process by *observer-analysts*. Our aim, based on our perspective as *practitioner-analysts,* is to contribute to a self-critical construction of better approaches to facilitation. We believe that, as well as having a desire to achieve positive political goals, empowering facilitation must be based on the do-it-yourself skills of a craftsperson, drawing on tacit understandings far from the critical distance of the conventional social researcher.

In much of the supposedly empowering participatory practice over the past thirty years, facilitators have contributed to the entrenchment of the very dominating authority that we could have, in theory, helped democratise. This is often because we have uncritically attempted to apply an off-the-shelf method of participation as if it were merely a technical procedure or research method.[2] This is in stark opposition to a concept of facilitation as a craft. Like any craft skill, facilitation requires a comprehensive apprenticeship rather than a handful of brief lessons. In facilitation this training has to be sufficiently broad for practitioners to know how to facilitate in a range of complex and usually highly politicised contexts.[3]

A useful perspective through which to understand facilitation is that of what Weinsten and Weinstein call 'intellectual bricolage', which they suggest was pioneered, though not named, by sociologist Georg Simmel.[4] Bricolage simply means construction using whatever was available at the time. The related French word bricoleur refers to a handyman or handywoman who makes use of the tools available to ensure he or she completes the task.

Inspired by Simmel, Weinsten and Weinstein observe that a process undertaken by an intellectual bricoleur 'is not always or even usually the same job that was initially undertaken and is uniquely structured by the set of pre-constrained elements that are selected from the treasury'.[5] Joe Kincheloe, Pete McLaren and Shirley Steinberg suggest that a bricolage perspective allows us to 'move beyond the blinds of particular disciplines and peer through a conceptual window to a new world of research and knowledge-production'.[6]

In a review about the use of the bricolage concept in critical research, Kincheloe *et al.* suggest that bricoleurs task themselves with 'uncovering the invisible artefacts of power and culture and documenting the nature of their influence'. Avoiding modes of reasoning that come from traditions of logical analysis, bricoleurs embrace complexity and reject standardised modes of knowledge production. They suggest that a bricoleur's 'interactions with the objects of their inquiries... are always complicated, mercurial, unpredictable and, of course, complex'.[7]

Kincheloe *et al.*'s analysis is core to understanding how good facilitation takes place in that they reject the practice of advance strategy planning. In lieu of such a rationalisation of the process, they suggest that 'bricoleurs enter into the research act as methodological negotiators'. Respecting the demands of the task at hand, bricolage 'resists its placement in concrete as it promotes its elasticity'. They suggest that better qualitative research will come from bricoleurs understanding the 'research method as also a technology of justification, meaning a way of defending what we assert we know and how we know it'.[8]

Like Kincheloe *et al.*, we suggest that the apprenticeship of facilitators, like critical researchers, involves allowing ourselves to step back from learning new methods in order to discuss concepts and develop a critical consciousness, a process that Paulo Freire famously called conscientization. 'Such a consciousness', they conclude, 'refuses the passive acceptance of externally imposed research methods that tacitly certify modes justifying knowledges that are decontextualised, reductionistic, and inscribed by dominant modes of power'. We, like most facilitators we have met, recognise a similar conscientization process is part of our own ongoing development as critically-minded facilitators of participatory processes.

A defining characteristic of grassroots-led processes with the potential to democratise authority is that they are established in order to resist or reconfigure a specific policy or its implementation by a dominating authority. The knowledge and authority of powerful institutions stem from their capacity to exert control over the gathering, interpretation and deployment of that knowledge. Creating spaces in which non-elites can have a voice – an essential part in the co-production of authority - not only challenges the validity of authoritative knowledge but can also undermine the legitimacy of those who deploy it.

Taking participation seriously inevitably risks conflict with organisations that have a vested interest in maintaining their existing dominance. Those institutions may take steps to respond by attempting to discredit the process. A response that utilises facilitation skills uncritically as a mere collection of methods has little chance to enter into a constructive dialogue with dominating authorities. However, we have found that adding the skills of a widely-experienced bricoleur can allow people whose voices have been marginalised to gain authority for their knowledge beyond what they could have previously thought possible.

Our experience acting as facilitators of participatory processes includes one set of events that took place in a particularly highly-charged political context – our co-facilitation with

Indian colleagues of the *Prajateerpu* hearings in 2001–02. In attempting to facilitate an empowering process, we aimed to achieve multiple objectives simultaneously. For example, we attempted the co-production of authority with communities whose knowledge had been marginalised, while building a democratic process of resistance to attempts by dominating powers to undermine the new authority that such a process created.

Prajateerpu was a participatory response to *Vision 2020*, a government-sponsored plan for the future of eighty million people in the Indian state of Andhra Pradesh. It was authored by McKinsey's, a US consultancy firm, based on their model for the future of rural development, based on global-trade and international moves towards industrial agriculture. In 2000 this global vision had been endorsed by the Government of Andhra Pradesh for this highly agricultural Indian state. It was also backed by the UK's Department for International Development (DFID) and the World Bank.

At the heart of the Vision was a radical strategy proposing a shift of 80% of farmers from land they currently farmed, along with a mechanising of agriculture and the introduction of genetically modified (GM) crops. With the livelihoods of their members and those of their families at stake, civil society groups called for a genuinely participatory process: Prajateerpu (literally meaning 'people's verdict' in Telegu). They asked that it address what they saw as the illegitimate authority attributed to a consultation process that had been overseen by the Government and foreign aid donors. DFID documents claimed that the agency had been part of

A member of the Prajateerpu ("People's Verdict") process questions a witness in Medak District, Andra Pradesh, India, 2001.

consultations with local farmers, but all the evidence from NGOs in the State suggested that only very large landowners had been consulted in meetings from which smallholder and marginal farmers had effectively been excluded.

Our involvement in this two year project took place while we were employed in two organisations: Tom at the Institute of Development Studies (IDS) and Michel at the International Institute for Environment and Development (IIED). IDS, the larger of the two organisations, is located on the campus of the University of Sussex but it is a separate organisation that is not part of the University. Its leadership had an ambivalent attitude towards participatory processes, a characteristic that was particularly important in what followed. IDS is a privatised government agency, retaining close personal and funding links to senior Whitehall officials, particularly at DFID.

Michel, then at IIED, was approached by Indian activist groups to undertake a participatory process. Using funds obtained from the Netherlands' Directorate-General for International Cooperation (DGIS) and the Rockefeller Foundation, we were able to support civil society groups from across Andhra Pradesh in co-designing a process that would enable the groups who would be most affected by vision 2020 to explore the consequences of this Vision and potential alternative visions for the future of the State's rural people.

We joined local collaborators in co-designing a participatory process of dialogue that would encompass multiple perspectives. We drew on our previous experience in order to co-design a process with our Indian partners that allowed our locally-based co-facilitators, speaking in dialects familiar to local farmers, to support the jury members to develop their analysis of the issues relevant to them and their communities.

Prajateerpu took place in the context of the dominating power of a State Government that had no means of entering into dialogue with smallholder farmers. The process enabled the knowledge of rural dwellers, informed by a deliberative process, to be applied and used in the cross examination of experts, many of whom were in a village setting for the first time. External experts presented different visions of the future of rural development in the State, but it was the jury who wrote the recommendations based on their own perspective, knowledge and analysis.

The eighteen members of *Prajateerpu* thus developed their own vision for rural development in the State that threw a wholly different light on development and was diametrically opposed to some of the core assumptions behind *Vision 2020.* Their vision was one of greater local autonomy and reviving crop varieties that had been wiped out due to recent changes in the State's agricultural policies. They stated that they had never seen all the foreign aid money, which they had learnt, through *Prajateerpu*, had been sent to their State to be used for communities like theirs. They had not been consulted about Vision 2020. In their report they made it clear that they didn't want any part of the plan to take place and that they had an alternative vision.

The process of organising and facilitating *Prajateerpu* saw us constantly adapting the process to changing circumstances. We took a bricoleur's approach to addressing the potential for those whose interests were threatened by Prajateerpu to accuse us of manipulating the process. We instituted an extensive range of safeguards that were enough to convince a range of stakeholders – from the State Government to Syngenta – to accept that the proceedings had been fair. Our Oversight Panel was convened by a retired Chief of the Supreme Court of India[9]

Director of the International Institute for Environment and Development, Nigel Cross, receives the Telegu language edition of the report of the Prajateerpu.

Despite the safeguards we instituted, DFID-India decided to challenge our report of the process, conveying their perspective in letters to our respective institute directors.[10] With its annual budget so dependent on governmental sources, IDS management took the unprecedented step of removing the report from its website and withdrew copies of the printed version. This was undertaken immediately without any process to review any flaws that may, or may not, have been present in the *Prajateerpu* report.

At this point our efforts seemed to have been in vain. Yet we believed we had co-facilitated a process that was fair and open. Despite being far superior to anything DFID had undertaken on the topic, the UK Government officials were, we believed, using their authority over IDS and other players to retain control of the policy space.

Together with our Indian colleagues, we decided to defend *Prajateerpu*'s transformative potential, in policy contexts both in India and internationally. We ensured our reply to DFID's criticisms was widely circulated. Our actions as participatory bricoleurs allowed the public exposure of the double standards existing at DFID and IDS. With our Indian collaborators we embarked on a creative campaign to defend the integrity of a process that had provided a platform for the informed views of some of the most marginalised rural people in India. It was not a comfortable experience for either of us.

We responded directly and publicly to the government criticisms of the censored jury report. Our whistle blowing on DFID's failure to implement its own policies promoting the use of community participation in the planning of development led to widespread media coverage and a global online campaign. This was among the factors causing DFID to pause to review its policies and gradually shift away from supporting McKinsey's original *Vision 2020*.[11] More importantly, it is one of many instances of facilitators being able to nurture the transformative power of participatory processes by a process that is best described as bricolage.

Our experience of being bricoleur-facilitators suggests that much more is needed for the participatory democratic model to succeed that the standard "principles of good practice" drawn up by various participation organisations in recent years.[12] We argue that such guidelines perpetuate a myth that giving communities a voice through participatory processes can be achieved simply by the application of a preconceived toolkit of methods.

In *Prajateerpu,* the use of bricolage in a complex and highly political process led to a partial transformation of authority, though not without ongoing controversy. Far from being the exception, our practical experience of participatory work over a combined total of forty years suggests that the way such processes democratise authority is more through craft-like processes rather than those based on rationalistic epistemologies.

The lack of dialogue between social scientists and practitioners of participatory processes is perhaps the biggest reason why facilitation has remained as a virtually-unexamined black-box for so long. In the current UK and global recession, facilitators have even less time and resources to undertake critical reflection, particularly when compared with those employed as professional researchers by universities and other research institutions. To enter the new age of participatory democracy that many authors in this book seek, we need to ensure that the comparatively generous resources for analysis available to us as researchers are shared with practitioners in order for further insights to be co-produced. If such dialogues could take place, both groups would be informed and inspired by diverse perspectives of the other. Together we can light more candles of participatory hope to offset the social disintegration promised by those who use their authority only to dominate.

---

[1] Davies, C. et al. (2006) *Citizens at the Centre: Deliberative Participation in Healthcare Decisions*, London: Policy Press.

[2] For example, see Involve (2010) People and Participation, London: Involve (accessed at http://www.involve.org.uk/wp-content/uploads/2011/03/People-and-Participation.pdf on 7 December 2012).

[3] Horton, M. (1998) *The Long Haul: An Autobiography*, New York: Teacher's College Press; Wagner, J. (2011) 'Ignorance in Educational Research: How Not Knowing Shapes New Knowledge', in P. Thomson & M. Walker (eds) *The Routledge Doctoral Student's Companion*, London: Routledge.

[4] Weinstein, D. & Weinstein, M. (2012) *Postmodern(ized) Simmel*. London: Routledge.

[5] Weinstein, D. & Weinstein, M. (2012) *Postmodern(ized) Simmel*, p.64

[6] Kincheloe, J. et al. (2011) 'Critical Pedagogy and Qualitative Research: Moving to the Bricolage', in N. Denzin & Y. S. Lincoln (eds) (2011) *The Sage Handbook of Qualitative Research*. New York: Sage.

[7] Kincheloe, J. et al. (2011) 'Critical Pedagogy and Qualitative Research: Moving to the Bricolage', p.168.

[8] Kincheloe, J. et al. (2011) 'Critical Pedagogy and Qualitative Research: Moving to the Bricolage', p.169.

[9] Pimbert, M. & Wakeford, T. (2003) 'Prajateerpu, Power and Knowledge: The Politics of Participatory Action Research in Development. Part I: Context, Process and Safeguards', *Action Research*, vol. 1, pp. 184–207.

[10] Wakeford, T. & Pimbert, M. (2004) 'Prajateerpu, Power and Knowledge: The Politics of Participatory Action Research in Development. Part 2: Analysis, Reflections and Implications', *Action Research*, vol. 2, pp. 25–46

[11] Kuruganti, K. et al. (2008) 'The People's Vision: UK and Indian Reflections on Prajateerpu', Participatory Learning and Action, vol. 58, pp. 11-17.

[12] For example, see National Consumer Council (2008) Deliberative public engagement: nine principles, London: National Consumer Council (accessed at http://www.involve.org.uk/wp-content/uploads/2011/03/Deliberative-public-engagement-nine-principles.pdf on 7 December 2012).

On Visiting Forgotten Tombs

Helen Nicholson

[F]or the growing good of the world is partly dependent on unhistoric acts; and that things are not so ill with you and me as they might have been, is half owing to the number who lived faithfully a hidden life, and rest in unvisited tombs.[1]

In the last line of *Middlemarch*, George Eliot offers a reflection on the life of Dorothea Brooke, whose sense of obligation led her to serve the dry scholarship of her husband Casaubon, but whose creativity and passion meant that she fell in love with Will Ladislaw's energy, idealism and cultural activism. For Eliot, a translator of Spinoza, Dorothea's inner conflict shows that human relationships must be understood emotionally and ethically, and in ways that challenged the conventional moral virtues of her time. It was her 'unhistoric acts' – acts that will never be written into official histories - that made a difference to the world, marking social change through a quiet poetics of participation.

The idea that political participation is a poetic act was, of course, codified by the Romantics and found further expression in Eliot's social realism. What Eliot understood was that an ethics of social participation is not only dependent on abstract ideals, imagination and vision – Shelley's argument in *A Defence of Poetry* - it is both sited and situated, enacted in the small and intimate moments of everyday life in which an idea or vision is turned to practical politics. Of course the only examples that we can know are those that have been documented by historians, passed down in folklore or across generations of family history, but many of us know that the actions of a good teacher, a kind aunt or helpful stranger changed or enhanced the course of a life. A good life, in this context, is not immortalised in either great poetry or grand monuments to heroic men, but is defined by how we go about our daily lives, our unremarkable habits and routines of life. The moment of death marks the beginning of being forgotten. People may be unremembered and their tombs unvisited, Eliot suggests, but their acts are all the more significant because they have participated in her optimistic vision of 'the growing good of the world' through small gestures and quotidian practices.

It is this sense of lives that are lived and forgotten that is perhaps felt most acutely in an abandoned graveyard; the dash that separates two dates on a tombstone symbolises, as the poet Sylvia Plath observed, the whole span of a life. Visiting unvisited tombs presses political questions about an everyday

ethics of participation, about what we are each doing in the dash – the dent marked in stone– the time between the date we already know and the unknown date that will balance the asymmetry. It is here that a poetics of participation might provide an opportunity to get a grip, at least temporarily, on life (and death) as a dance between the human and non-human, in which the materiality of existence is marked as temporary and contingent. Nowhere is this dance more poetic and more physical than in a patch of land where the dead are buried.

A poetics of participation that acknowledges the dance between the human and the nonhuman, that recognises the ethical force of unheroic and unhistoric acts, requires a new set of pedagogical vocabularies, and new ways of learning. I am searching for a poetic pedagogy that understands that 'the growing good of the world' is an organic process, experienced both intellectually and in the unreflexive practices of everyday life, as enactment, embodiment and inhabitation. This moves beyond the dialecticism associated with conventional Marxist critical pedagogies or humanist theories of social constructivist learning. It opens questions about how the values and practices of educators and activists who have been long associated with equality might be recast for the contemporary work. Perhaps one of the most obvious examples might be found in the work of the theatre director Augusto Boal, who has influenced generations of activists. Boal's ways of working were influenced by Paulo Friere's idea that education should aim to makes people 'more human', and his trademark 'Theatre of the Oppressed' was build on this premise.[2] Theatre of the Oppressed often involves actors dramatising social issues, resolved through debate with the audience, who are asked to try out their solutions in improvised performance. Boal describes these people as 'spectators', and it is interesting in this context that it is the spectator whom Boal casts as 'inhuman'; spectatorship, in this conceptualisation, equates with passivity, and a lack of participation in Boal's particular idea of a performative pedagogy provides him sufficient evidence for people's inhumanity. This opens a political gap between rhetoric and practice, and in all the many theatre-events inspired by Boal's pedagogy I have witnessed across the world, I have rarely seen participation that is equitable. It is flawed, often, by two issues; first, that it is led by theatre-makers, facilitators or educators who may have very different backgrounds from their audiences, and who bring their own particular vision of 'humanity' to the performance that may well be at odds with the local community. Performers command the power of attention, and the dramaturgical structure may have the effect of coercing an audience into particular points of view. It is unsurprising, in this context, that Boal's methods have been applied to corporate management training as well as political activism. Second, it takes a particular kind of courage to get up in front of an audience and improvise in role, and it is almost inevitably the case that audience members who are already confident in this setting volunteer to participate. The first may be recognisably prejudicial, albeit unintentionally so, and the second also fails to acknowledge the affective force of atmosphere, mood and environment, of human and nonhuman interaction.

The unvisited tomb, and the dash between the dates, serve as metaphors that prompt questions about what is meant by an everyday ethics of participation. In Eliot's novel, understanding how to participate in the world is represented as a daily challenge, often fraught with contradiction and emotional tension. As Ben Anderson and Paul Harrison suggest, "we come to know and enact a world from inhabiting it, from becoming attuned to its differences and juxtapositions, from a training of our senses, dispositions and expectations".[3] This way of thinking represents a radical inversion of social constructivist pedagogies, in which meaning is projected onto the (socially constructed) world. A poetics of participation depends not only on thought, but also involves training the senses. Neither poetry nor participation are intrinsically morally beneficial, but the poetic can capture and magnify the small details of life, pausing on ambiguities, and turning its intimacies and patterns of living into metaphor and symbol. The poetic life is 'distilled', to borrow the words of African American poet Gwendolyn Brooks; it holds the world still, allowing us to pay attention. This affective process of observation and inhabitation invites new insights, as George Eliot notes with characteristic candour, illuminating the aesthetic and performative patterns of ordinary life that are necessary for imagining social change, but are sometimes too painful to bear:

If we had a keen vision and feeling of all ordinary human life, it would be like hearing the grass grow and the squirrel's heart beat, and we should die of that roar which lies on the other side of silence. As it is, the best of us walk about well wadded with stupidity.[4]

---

[1] Eliot, G. (1874) *Middlemarch*, Harmondsworth: Penguin Books,
[2] Boal, A. (1979) *Theatre of the Oppressed* London: Pluto Press.
[3] Anderson, B. & Harrison, P. (eds.) (2010) *Taking Place: Non-Representational Theories and Geography*, Farnham: Ashgate, p.9.
[4] Eliot, G. (1874) *Middlemarch*, p.145.

Participating With Objects

Tehseen Noorani

"...the name is the thing ... and the true name is the true thing. To speak the name is to control the thing." Mr. Underhill, in Ursula le Guin, *The Rule of Names.*

On Sattins Island, to name something correctly – to speak its 'true name' – is to achieve absolute power over it. What Ursula le Guin explores in her short story of Mr. Underhill, and through her more expansive Earthsea trilogy, offers insights for the analysis of mastery and power. Indeed, the idea of true names has existed for millennia and can be traced through many cultural histories.[1] Those of us interested in participatory democracy can feel uncomfortable with the idea of putting names on things, as though doing so somehow disturbs a presumption of equality or sameness between us. However, if naming has power, perhaps rather than refusing to name, we should incorporate a deeper appreciation of the power of naming into our understanding of how participation works. After all, participation is both 'a work' and needs to be made 'to work'. The idea of true names offers a clue – they only 'work' because they accurately describe a thing. What, then, is the importance of this process of correctly naming for practices of empowerment?

To participate is to come together to act, and creating knowledge is a vital aspect of acting – we learn about what we are doing, and we experiment with what we can do. Most of us would agree that participatory knowledges emerge through dialogue and contestation between actors who come together. According to one theory of participation, this involves the formation of a new, collective unity, comprised of individuals and groups that are able to act as a new actor and develop a distinct self-awareness. This theory brings the idea of participation into proximity with a sense of 'communion'. We see it, for example, in the Frereian approach to participation. The subject and object of participation come together and become indissoluble in the participatory experience.[2] A related theory of participation emphasises how the participating actors *themselves* cannot be anticipated prior to the moment they encounter one another. Instead, they emerge through particular encounters. This participatory ideal requires that participants name themselves, rather than being named by others. Putting these two theories together, it could be argued that participation occurs when individuals and groups rename themselves in the development of new forms of collective subjectivity, and in so doing, make new claims upon the ways in which things are seen, understood and done.

However, I want to draw attention to a different way of approaching what is meant by 'participation'. Here rather than unity or communion, *objectification* is vital in the production of effective participatory knowledges. To 'objectify' means to treat as an object, which includes endowing with the corresponding power of an object.[3] The process of objectification is about creating objects that have the power to 'object'. They have boundaries; they push back. This is the beginning of a relationship that yields knowledge. In a sense this is obvious – without objects we cannot act, for acting implies both *to act upon* something, and *to be acted upon* by something. To be provoked, be advised by and control others; to shape, steer, break and make requests of others – all these permutations presuppose a distance that distinguishes subjects of participation from their objects. It begins by being able to name an object.

What's more, while participation exists as a problem for the *collective*, parts at other levels than 'groups' of 'individual people' are also able to part-icipate. Participation occurs both for the individual and within the individual. The varieties of participatory practices might take place between you and me, but they hold equally between me and the 'old me', and even between sub-parts of you (all) and sub-parts of me. The goal is not for all parts to become equally powerful by flattening out relations of power. It is for the parties to be able to work upon one another, creating more powerful relations, increasing both individual and collective capacities to affect and be affected.

Once we distinguish that which we can act on – and which can act on us – from ourselves, we are able to interact with it, developing our relations with it in a 'dance of agency'.[4] We often get to know objects by engaging with them and learning more about their limits. Like children playing with toys, we sometimes understand and trust an object only once we've broken it, thereby overstepping its limits. Taking such a material approach to knowledge helps to avoid opposing the world 'out there' with the mind 'within', but instead to focus on the project of better understanding the relations in which we find ourselves always and already participating.

Naming is a powerful tool of participation because it is a way of creating an object and/or fixing the boundaries between subject and object. Wittgenstein demonstrated that there is no such thing as a private language; to communicate is necessarily to connect. We develop our shared languages in many ways – naming a mutual concern; naming an illness, condition or affective state we resist; naming ourselves as a point of resistance or transformation; naming that thing between us ('thank God *someone* said it!') and other such objects that can then be worked upon; naming the boundaries of these objects; naming our strengths and capacities; naming the safe space where we can do our work. In this sense, participation is not just about naming ourselves as a given or emerging unity, but about working upon the myriad differences outside, between and within ourselves. It is about the creation of *somethings*, just as much as it is about the emergence of *someones*. The act of naming delineates, defines, bounds and distinguishes what can be worked upon and with.

From fantasy to folklore to the rules of democratic parliaments, all cultures are full of examples of how naming something allows us to get a hold over it.[5] In pursuit of equality we may prefer to not make distinctions, but this can be dangerous. Not naming can leave unacknowledged, and thereby obfuscate, influences that remain as *unnamed powers*. It is important for participatory interventions to be designed in ways that allow any and all of us to challenge the claims to equality that can prevent effective knowledge construction.

We can witness boundary-making in the countless participation handbooks and manuals littering the field of participation. The boundaries or distances between subject and object can be temporal, spatial, material, ideational, cognitive or affective. For instance, the juries of citizens' juries are separated from the experts that testify before them in specific and time-bound slots.[6] Juries are effective, not in spite of being, but because, they are insulated from the outside world when discussing issues and deepening a shared knowledge-base. Jury members understand themselves as neutral and non-partisan, sorting and sifting the opinions of the other, *more interested*, parties. The popular participatory technique of Open Space Technology demands that participants find themselves engaged in pedagogic activity at all times, thereby delineating the possibilities of their relationship to their environment – according to the 'Law of Two Feet', they must not sit idly.[7] The mental healthcare technique of Open Dialogue illustrates the empowering 'openness' that emerges from proscribing where and when the person at the centre of concern cannot be talked about.[8] Here, rather than speak openly whenever and wherever they want, participants must reserve communication about the person for sessions where the person is present. In this way, the safe space of Open Dialogue is maintained only by closing down the possibility of speech elsewhere. In all three of these examples, the arcs of participatory processes both presume and create certain boundaries.

Part of the challenge of participatory initiatives is for participants to accept that while they may be equally capable of learning, how much each participant understands at any time will be different. When this happens, different forms of expertise can be celebrated and maximized in their contact with one another. In one UK-based example, members of Bristol's Stepping Out Theatre Company spoke about how they have developed a series of strategies and techniques for overcoming difficult problems that emerge in the course of planning and performing – a kind of a science of engaging with, while perhaps not solving, problems – a 'problematology'.[9] In another example, the Mad Hatters of Bath reported how a particular member who was prone to highs and lows of mood discovered that they were very good at intensely 'casing the space' at participatory events for a few hours, but then would need to rest and recover so as not to burn out.[10] Rather than understand these two groups as correcting or compensating for deficiencies under some kind of 'deficit model' of mental distress, we can understand them as creating new techniques and capacities that all of us are able to learn from, adapt and adopt in our own ways. The knowledge they gain is useful to individual members and also to the group as a whole. It is a practical knowledge that exists in a range of capacities.

Of course, in one sense participation demands that we keep things open, in order that we may move forward in a contingent and democratic manner. However, participatory initiatives that are too open do not achieve very much – at the very least, we might agree on a minimal set of stakes, concerns and/or problems, which then has a crucial grounding role. This suggests an *ecological* view of participation. Too many objects can leave actors uncertain and reactive. Too few objects can lead to the participatory collective being prematurely celebrated as a unity, but one that understands neither itself (including all its internal differences) nor its capacities. The subtle craft of participation requires assembling sufficiently rich ecologies for the various agents of participation to begin building knowledges of their relations and their individual and collective capacities.

The goal of objectification is not to simply create objects but to *engage* them – to work upon them and to be worked upon by them. The participatory journey creates subjects with ever-greater knowledges and capacities to affect and be affected by the objects of their environments. Objectification, including boundary-formation through naming, is useful for planning and conducting participatory activities that create objects for the purpose of getting work done. As Mr. Underhill explains, naming is not an end, a solution, but a means for us to attain greater control over our situations.

Argyris noted in the 1970s that in all learning processes, the creation of objects, names and boundaries is generational. First, we work with particular ecologies of relations and objects, and then we overturn them and reinstate better ones.[11] We never fully understand our relations with the objects of experience. They continually surprise us and whenever they do, we wish we knew 'then' what we know 'now'. Objectification is permanently replacing itself – it is crucial to the beginning and end of cycles of inquiry. Refusing to objectify stalls effective participatory learning by preventing objects from being able to push back. On the contrary, attending to how objectification occurs, through such techniques as naming, separating, forming and testing boundaries, helps us in clarifying participation-as-craft. Participation then is not simply about opposing reification in the name of something else. The good does not operate according to different laws than the bad. We can begin by recognising that if objectification lurks at the heart of power, then it must also be at the heart of our practices of empowerment.

---

1 http://tvtropes.org/pmwiki/pmwiki.php/Main/IKnowYourTrueName. Last accessed January 30th, 2013.

2 For example, Thomas, R., Whybrow, K. and Scharber, C. (2011) 'A Conceptual Exploration of Participation. Section II: Participation as Engagement in Experience – An Aesthetic Perspective', *Educational Philosophy and Theory*, 44(7), pp. 746-759.

3 http://www.merriam-webster.com/dictionary/objectify. Last accessed January 30th, 2013.

4 Pickering, A. (1995) *The Mangle of Practice: Time, agency, and science*, Chicago: University of Chicago Press.

5 http://tvtropes.org/pmwiki/pmwiki.php/Main/IKnowYourTrueName.

---

6 http://jefferson-center.org/what-we-do/citizen-juries. Last accessed January 30th, 2013.

7 http://www.openspaceworld.com/users_guide.htm. Last accessed January 30th, 2013.

8 Seikkula, J., Aaltonen, J., Alakare, B., Haarakangas, K., Keranen, J. and Lehtinen, K. (2006) 'Five-year experience of first-episode nonaffective psychosis in open-dialogue approach: Treatment principles, follow-up outcomes, and two case studies', *Psychotherapy Research*, 16(2), pp. 214-228. Available at http://bit.ly/Am67HE (last accessed January 30th 2013).

9 Interview with Stepping Out Theatre Company, Bristol, April 2012. See http://www.steppingouttheatre.co.uk (last accessed January 30th, 2013)

10 Interview with Mad Hatters of Bath, April 2012.

11 Argyris, C. (1976) *Increasing Leadership Effectiveness*, New York: Wiley.

Futures of an Unlived Past

Julian Brigstocke

'What are the roots that clutch, what branches grow Out of this stony rubbish?' [1]

Sensory Garden

Who should participate in the making of the future? Much effort goes into inventing ways of giving voices to the young, the inheritors of the earth. But perhaps the dead, too, should participate in the future. The dead have had their time, some might argue; it is time for a new generation to take over. And yet bleak histories of injustice and oppression make it clear that many people never *did* have their time. They ran out of time before gaining a chance to shape time.

The question, anyway, is irrelevant. The dead *do* participate in the future. Not just in the bodies they pass down, or the wealth, or the memories; but also in the material settings that they shaped, and which persist today. Our cities, for example, are collective bodies that create possibilities for living in the future; but they have (often) been designed, built and modified by the dead. Cities, collective capacities for the future, are also stony spirits from the past.

Rubble

Plymouth, UK, 1941. Total devastation.[2] The city's past is crumbling into the sea and the soil. Amidst the ashes, smoke and burnished bricks, people dance along the clifftop of Plymouth Hoe, shifting their bodies in defiance of an enemy beyond sight, over the waves and above the clouds. An echo, across the centuries, of Francis Drake's game of bowls on these same cliffs, waiting for the winds to turn before setting forth against the Spanish fleet.

"Even the Hoe had never known such evenings as those when the blitz had spent its fury. Inland, stricken Plymouth stretched across its hills, there was a grim lattice-work of stripped and shattered roofs; wrecked St Andrews stood by the ruin of the Guildhall walls. Above this chaos the sound of Military band music drifted over the embers of central Plymouth. It came from the Hoe. Tired people, streaming in thousands through Lockyer Street, answered the call to listen and join in the dance led by the indefatigable Lady Mayoress. Here the city, throwing off its cares in one symbolic gesture, laughed a siege to scorn."[3]

Station Road, Keyham, Plymouth, 1940s. © Plymouth and West Devon Record Office 616/114/4/3.

Phoenix

A mythic moment, perhaps. A *founding* myth, a modernist reworking of Romulus and Remus. The main avenue of the rebuilt city was almost called Phoenix Way. This makes Plymouth almost unique in the UK, where cities are usually described in languages of centuries-long organic growth, not vocabularies of founding and re-founding.

Yet the very possibility of democratic participation, writes Hannah Arendt, relies on collective acts of re-founding.[4] We moderns have found the revolutionary, destructive side of democracy, she argues, much easier to come to grips with than its foundational, constructive side. Political freedom requires collective assertions of new collective institutions and spaces.

The destruction of Plymouth, by creating the necessity of a new act of re-founding, briefly created a new opening for democracy. This opening was closed off again soon enough. But walking along the windy central roads of the city – neglected monuments to a broken promise – it is possible to discern the material traces of a post-war social democratic dream, a unique moment in British democracy: the engineering of a well-planned, ordered, protective society, supported by a strong and democratic state. The reconstruction of Plymouth is a less well-known counterpart to the founding of the National Health Service. It was fiercely fought for by such political luminaries as Lord Reith, Michael Foot and Nancy Astor (Plymouth's Member of Parliament, the first female MP). It was to be a concrete experiment in a new aesthetics of freedom.

If the dancing on the Hoe gave Plymouth its symbolic re-founding, it is Abercrombie and Paton Watson's document *A Plan For Plymouth* which brought together the symbolic and the practical. Perhaps one of the most important, if somewhat under-recognized, British planning documents of the 20th century, it imagined a new city based on a sense of community that had been reinvigorated by the war. It described a new city free of the blights of overcrowding and traffic log-jams. 'The city', it suggested, should be the focal point of the diffused rays of the many separate beams of life'. 'During the war years', it went on, 'there has been a decided trend of public opinion back to the spirit of the community, and increasingly insistent demands are being made for better and more efficient use of the land to the benefit of the people as a whole'.[5] It imagined a city that would encourage participation in community and democratic institutions. Created through entirely non-participatory means, it imagined an architecture *for* participation. It exemplified a non-participatory politics of participation.

TV Screen

The city's success in developing its plan in the face of huge obstacles has been credited to the extraordinary authority that the Plymouth Plan quickly acquired. Whitehall bureaucrats quickly realised that the plan had become a local 'Magna Carta', and could not be easily interfered with.[6] It enjoyed widespread popular support. The authoritativeness of the plan can be partly attributed to a canny publicity campaign – most importantly, a television documentary made by Jill Craigie, called *The Way We Live*. Following a (fictitious) working class Plymouth family, the film explained the reasoning and utopian ambition of the plan and the improved housing, community and living conditions that it aimed to foster. In addition, 'a second crucial factor was the immediate engagement of an external expert whose judgment would be hard to question and whose ideas were not easily challenged'.[7] This raises a recurrent question – what Arendt calls 'the *great* question' – in political thought. If a new foundation has to be created, it can only be founded by people with no authority to do so. But if they have no authority to do so, how can the new authority be grounded? [8] Perhaps it is impossible to create a participatory democracy through participatory means. The solution developed here, in any case, was to draw on the external authority of a famous urban planner.

Utopia

Plymouth's architecture is not well loved.[9] It is, after all, deeply out of keeping with the times. It could hardly be less fashionable. The kind of strict zoning it maintains (carefully separating out commercial, industrial and residential space) was abandoned long ago in most cities. Abercrombie's *Plan For Plymouth* was at once the first and the last Beaux-Arts city plan in Britain.[10] One might even say that of all British cities, it is Plymouth that has the greatest affinity to Paris. But, as Walter Benjamin once observed, the real animating spirit of political practice can perhaps only really be seen when their dreams have faded and the images have fallen out of fashion.[11] When fashions have lost their intoxicating power (the ephemeral atmosphere of novelty), the utopias they imagine come more clearly into view.

Stone

The use of Portland Stone for many of the buildings in the new city centre was controversial. In the *Plan*, Abercrombie had intended to use the most modern of construction materials: steel and reinforced concrete made from local limestone aggregate, thereby blending old and new. In the event, a less radically 'modern' solution was adopted. The use of Portland Stone also fulfilled a number of practical and financial motives, such as the need to keep the Portland quarry in operation.

Plymouth's buildings were designed to be reused and reshaped: 'to be infinitely flexible and adaptable to all passing fashions'.[12] The stone buildings were (and remain) high quality, long life, and low energy. They were not intended to be beautiful in and of themselves; rather, beauty was to come through the creative *use* of them, which would bring new and more transitory adornments. The aesthetic qualities of the city, that is, were to be created through citizens' participation in the production of its spaces. The contrast with recently built shopping centres such as Drake Circus is striking. Designed for instant impact, the embodiment of fashion, they soon look antiquated and absurd.

However, this aspiration went largely unrealized. As the architect Jeremy Gould tells us, 'Portland Stone buildings require intense coloured shopfronts, signs and blinds for contrast and visual interest. In the 1950s, this is exactly what they got, but later, the need was forgotten in a rash of commercialism and the balance between neutral background and positive shopfronts was obscured by the feeble design of both.'[13] Yet this indicates that possibilities still exist for living a new past of this unfashionable present. Rather than heeding the cries to demolish Plymouth's spaces once again, legitimising a new round of 'creative destruction', perhaps what is needed is a politics of re-inhabiting these spaces, creatively re-activating their faded potential, wrenching these spaces from the blandness of commodification.

Litter Bin

The centrepiece of the *Plan for Plymouth* was a long, monumental avenue running from the railway station to the Hoe. Subsequent landscaping, however, dramatically reduced the impact of this grand boulevard, as well as other streets. Although designed for traffic, the city centre was pedestrianized, making the streets feel empty and far too wide. To fill them, various pieces of 'civic junk' have been placed in them, camouflaging the potential of these spaces. 'On a wet windy day, when the seats are unusable, the suburban planting bedraggled, the crowds have not appeared and the wind has emptied the litter bins, they take on an uncomfortable bleakness which is unique to Plymouth'.[14] With the completion of the commodification of the city, participation of people in the production of space has been replaced by the participation of *waste*.

Madame Sosostris

There is something faintly archaic about the current surge of interest in participatory democracy. This archaism isn't the apparent nostalgia amongst some theorists of participation for the slave democracy of Ancient Greence. Rather, it is a nostalgia for democracy itself - a sudden and passionate rediscovery of democratic life that is linked to a shivering premonition of its death.

Democracy is a commitment to a plastic future - to the possibility of grasping hold of time and shaping it according to the will of the people. Yet it is being saturated with the dismal prophecies of dead-eyed fortune-tellers. Economists, accountants, politicians and scientists announce to us that we have sold the future, burdening ourselves and our children with barely recoverable economic and environmental debts.

With the future shut off, it is time to learn better the craft of participating in the unlived futures of the past. Our future is disappearing into a continuous present; but pasts can always be remade, relived, reshaped. Democracy today requires the participation of the dead, the forgotten and the discarded, enabling us to improvise new pathways along the barbed knots of time.

'That corpse you planted last year in your garden,
Has it begun to sprout? Will it bloom this year?'[15]

---

[1] T.S. Eliot, *The Waste Land.*

[2] Plymouth suffered the worst war damage of all cities in England, with 3500 destroyed buildings, 70,000 damaged buildings, 900 citizens killed, 2000 injured, and 20,000 people displaced. Gould, Jeremy (2000) *Plymouth Planned: The Architecture of the Plan for Plymouth 1943 – 1962*, Bath: Jeremy and Caroline Gould Architects.

[3] Viscount Astor (1943) 'Introduction', in Paton Watson, J. & Abercrombie, P. *A Plan for Plymouth: The Report Prepared for the City Council,* Plymouth: Pymouth City Council, p. v.

[4] Arendt, Hannah (1963) *On Revolution*. Penguin.

[5] Paton Watson & Abercrombie, *A Plan for Plymouth,* p. 28.

[6] Essex, S. & Brayshay, M. (2008) 'Boldness diminished? The postwar battle to replan a bomb damaged provincial city', *Urban History*, 35(3), 437-461.

[7] Essex & Brayshay, 'Boldness diminished?'.

[8] See Honig, B. (1991) 'Declarations of Independence: Arendt and Derrida on the Problem of Founding a Republic', *The American Political Science Review*, 85(1), p. 85.

[9] A minor furore broke out, for example, when the Civic Centre was granted listed status in 2007, preventing its planned demolition.

[10] This observation is made in Gould, *Plymouth Planned.*

[11] Benjamin, Walter. *The Arcades Project.*

[12] Gould, *Plymouth Planned,* p. 105.

[13] Gould, *Plymouth Planned,* p. 107.

[14] Gould, *Plymouth Planned,* p. 106.

[15] T.S. Eliot, *The Waste Land.*

Problem Three

Participatory Democracy is a Struggle Against Privatization

Participation as Performance Sells

Helen Nicholson

Participation is performative, and it sells. Shops, restaurants, bars, petrol stations, hospitals and whole cities are 'themed', with the aim of providing consumers with a memorable experience that will lure them to spend money. The experience is carefully staged, but the story is left incomplete without us, as actors, completing it. We are asked to follow branded products on twitter, consulted over new lines and, despite tax controversy, Starbucks describe their followers as a 'family'. Participation also sells art, and it is significant in this context that the performance *You Me Bum Bum Train*, performed as part of the 2012 Cultural Olympiad, was marketed on their website in the following way:

"In an exhilarating, participatory adventure, you are the sole audience member, a passenger who journeys through a maze of live scenes. You will be catapulted into unimaginable situations before being returned to the outside world, breathless, invigorated and left wanting more."[1]

This sense of incompleteness is filled with the desire to participate, to buy into the lifestyle and to want more, with the allure of consultation with opinions and tastes that matter. Capitalism depends on this combination of desire and consumption.

There is, then, nothing inherently good about participation, if notions of 'goodness' are defined in terms of equality and social justice. But it is the political pliability of participation, both as a concept and a social practice, which makes it so seductive. Participation invokes the language and practices of theatre –we are sold stuff through spectacle, role, script, design, sound, music, image – each element more often associated with making theatre and social activism rather than shopping and cooking. I am drawn to Mauyra Wickstom's analysis of consumerism, *Performing Consumers*, in which she makes a powerful case for the role of the imagination in the process of consumption.[2] She argues that we are seduced by the environment created by different brands – she calls these 'brandscapes' - that sell products through experiences, in which we imagine ourselves to be different from how we actually are. Some shopping Malls, for example, describe themselves as a 'village', thereby simultaneously promoting a sense of belonging and consumer aspiration. The idea of playing a role and imagining ourselves to be different, so central to practices of participatory performance associated with the political Left, has been appropriated and called an 'experience economy'.

So what has happened to art in a culture in which the experience economy is so pervasive? The social turn in theatre[3] increasingly invites spectators to interact with the event of the performance. And arguably the seriously cool, metropolitan theatre crowd are more likely to be found at 'immersive' performances in derelict warehouses, tunnels and rooftops that in conventional theatre spaces, where the dramaturgical structure means that it is unclear who is the producer and consumer of the work of art. This relational and participatory aesthetic at the same time as proliferated with new forms of participation extending artists' (and audiences') repertoire. This kind of performativity sells, as pop-up theatres and pop-up restaurants satisfy the desire for new affective experiences. It trades on temporality and participation, captured by the ever-growing market for festivals.

An example might demonstrate the politically ambiguous relationship between participation and performance. The London International Theatre Festival (LIFT) in 2010 included a mobile composition by Dan Jones, *Music for Seven Ice-Cream Vans*. This musical composition was intended to be played by seven customised vintage ice cream vans, each of which contributed one section of the melody as it processed through the streets. The nostalgic novelty of this musical motorcade started at the pop-up LIFT venue in Canning Town, we chased the sound – glimpsing one or more of the ice cream vans that were touring the housing estates, each adding their chimes to the street composition. An international festival is not an entirely 'local' audience, and we made a motley crew of metropolitan arty-types, artists from overseas, people who had performed at other LIFT events. Most local people seemed scarcely to notice the cavalcade of pied-piper vans but others paused as they passed, looking up from their Saturday evening activities. On the one hand, this performative encounter with *Music for Seven Ice-Cream Vans* might be read as an example of a ludic city which, in the 1960s, was associated with social revolution. Certainly the playful tactic of enticing us to chase sound around the streets of Canning Town could be seen as making audiences playful explorers, but there was no sense of revolution. Another reading, however, would attend to the embodied and sensory affects of sound, how the effort to capture and listen to the music enables audiences to focus attention on the aurality of London's urban ecologies. It frames the sound theatrically, so that we might listen more carefully and reflect on its affect. The sonorous event-space offered by the seven ice cream vans required us to participate as an attuned 'earwitnesses' in the performance, a term Dee Heddon coined to suggest the performance of hearing, adding another ecological register to the experience of being in Canning Town.[4]

So how far is this form of aesthetic participation indebted to, or different from, the commodified experience economy? My suggestion is that they share the same affective pull, fostered by similar dramaturgical devices, and that this seduction requires a new political vigilance. Performance theory can open up questions of value, not least by interrogating the ways in which both consumption and 'art' lie at the performative intersection between embodiment, institution, practice and ideology. The experience economy promises to transform lives, to generate aspiration and effect social change, language that is familiar to activist artists. It is time for socially engaged artists to shed this set of vocabularies, and define their participatory practices in aesthetic and affective terms, and more precisely.

---

[1] http://festival.london2012.com/events/9000964050. Accessed 29/812.

[2] Wickstrom, M. (2006) Performing Consumers: Global Capital and its theatrical seductions New York and London: Routledge.

[3] The social turn in theatre has been elegantly described by Shannon Jackson (2011) *Social Works: Performing art, supporting publics,* London: Routledge

[4] Heddon, Deirdre (2010): The Horizon of Sound Soliciting the Earwitness, *Performance Research*, 15:3, pp. 36-42.

Participation in (A Time of) Crisis

Patrick Bresnihan

Early on in his novel, *The Grapes of Wrath*, John Steinbeck describes a scene in which officials from the bank come to repossess a farm in Oklahoma. The prelude to this confrontation is not described but we are told that the land has turned to dust. Most of the cotton farmers, and their families, did not profit from this ecological exploitation. But as times became hard and the production dwindled they were forced to borrow from the bank. As the cotton crops continued to fail the farmers were forced to borrow again. Now the land was dead and the farmers were left with no way of making an income and a debt to the bank. When the bank officials arrive to make good their debt they tell the farmers that they have to leave their homes and their land. The farmers cry out that it is their land. But the bank officials are not for moving:

We're sorry. It's not us. It's the monster. The bank isn't like a man.

Yes, but the bank is only made of men.

No, you're wrong there- quite wrong there. The bank is something else than men. It happens that every man in a bank hates what the bank does, and yet the bank does it. The bank is something more than men, I tell you. It's a monster. Men made it, but they can't control it.[1]

The bank does not operate like a man. It acts from cold calculation. It does not feel the memory of generations or the knowledge of place. It extends credit to a farmer under pressure not because it is kind and generous but because it exists to make a profit. The farmer was never going to be able to repay that debt. But the bank has no problem dispossessing the farmer and his family, and taking over the land. The house is bulldozed and the land is re-organized for new forms of production and the memory of the farmer and his family is erased.

This monster is alive and well today. However, unlike in the 1930s the issuing of credit and the accumulation of debt has become more entwined with the way our economy operates and the way our society is being undermined.

The withering of the welfare state since the 1970s has meant that access to credit has increasingly become the only way for large sections of the population to access basic social goods such as housing (mortgages), education (student loans) and transport (car loans). Those with no credit history, no secure income, no hope of repaying, have been extended the 'helping' hand of credit. Access to this credit is controlled by private banks and financial institutions (rather than democratically elected and accountable governments) who come to own our futures through the dominion of debt. Perhaps the clearest example of this dynamic and its consequences is the housing market. The expansion of the mortgage market allowed private banks to extend credit to the most vulnerable in society, enabling them to buy their own houses. This required the expansion of the financial system in general as new ways of absorbing, managing and commodifying the growing amounts of high-risk debt emerged. This was considered 'progress'... *private home ownership for everyone!*

But what happened when the bubble burst? In the wake of the property related financial crisis home owners, many of whom were already struggling to make payments in a stuttering economy, were left with greatly devalued properties and an inflated mortgage debt that they were unable to pay. These were not the people governments decided to bail out. Instead they stood by the banks, ensuring that credit would still flow, that the life force of money would not dry up. This effectively turned a private debt crisis into a sovereign debt crisis. Now governments, such as Greece and Ireland, are in the same position as heavily indebted individuals. Default beckons. Only the intervention of the European Central Bank and the International Monetary Fund have prevented this, by once again channelling billions of Euros into the hands of international bondholders and financiers.

The terms of the bailouts have meant violent austerity measures imposed on citizens already mired in their own personal debt and a precarious job market. Savage cuts in public services and welfare, privatizations and tax increases, represent an unprecedented act of dispossession inflicted by elected representatives on their own people: the transfer of public wealth to private banks and bondholders.

Financial Debt has become so much a part of our economic reality that the tragic consequences playing out before us are explained as the unfortunate consequences of reckless borrowing and irresponsible individual behaviour. This moralizing appears to justify the everyday injustice of some people eating out of bins while others collect bigger bonuses. It obscures the economic dynamics which have made financial debt the dead-beating heart of contemporary capitalism. It is both deadening and life-giving in that powerful financial institutions increasingly control access to money (life support for chronically stagnant western economies) while operating outside of the actual activities which produce goods and services. The monster does nothing to enrich the land or city from which it ultimately extracts its payments. It is not interested in stable jobs or decent wages. It is external to all life, except the life of money.

The consequences of this logic are reminiscent of 1930s Oklahoma on a far bigger scale. Just as the crops failed in Oklahoma and the farmers could not meet their loans, so the property-related financial crash left many with debts to pay and no means to pay it. Just as the lands of Oklahoma were left desiccated and unlivable, so too have parts of our cities become like urban dustbowls: the price of rent forcing out all but the wealthiest; neighborhoods boarded up; developments left unfinished or empty, and, as in Oklahoma, a growing number of the dispossessed left homeless and precarious. The monster does not shed a tear.

We work and we borrow in order to work and to borrow. This everyday cycle of fear and frustration is shared by students facing a desolate job market; home owners struggling to pay vastly inflated mortgages; precarious workers, all of us, who are forced to borrow to maintain a decent standard of life. As these fears mount and inequalities multiply it is not surprising that questions arise out of anger; questions which begin to ask how we can participate in a different world free from the burden of debt and a future of precarity.

But where can we bring our petitions? Where can we make our voices heard? The onslaught of austerity has made it clear whose side elected governments are on. The gap between the needs and interests of the people and the interests of private banks and financial institutions supported by political elites is widening. This gap is seemingly unbridgeable through existing channels of participation.

The immediate response to this apparent impasse is anger and depression. Before shooting himself in Syntagma Square the 77 year old ex-pharmacist, Dimitris Christoulas, whose pension was wiped out by the austerity measures, wrote: "I can find no other solution than to put an end to my life before I start sifting through garbage cans for my food." This is the tragic outcome of financial debt and state imposed austerity, yet it hardly made a ripple in the parliaments of Europe- in stark contrast to the urgency created when the high-priests of finance - the credit rating agencies - make pronouncements on sovereign debt. The only conclusion to draw from this is that people do not count for anything. They are, again, the 'swinish multitude' placed outside spaces and times of decision-making and wealth production. To paraphrase the sociologist Richard Sennett: 'the system is not broken - indeed it is working extremely well - it is just that the majority are excluded from it.'

But even in the nihilism of suicide there is the dignity of refusal. The refusal to accept the subordination of social life to financial profit. A refusal of the economic and political system that is cracking under the weight of its own contradictions. And from this refusal springs creation, the opening up of new possibilities for participation. As well as personal tragedies and violence the refusal to accept the burden of the crisis has produced new experiments in political participation and social commons in squares and streets around the world. Navarinou Park, Milbank, Tahrir square, Syntagma Square, Puerta del Sol, Wall Street, the streets of Quebec. All these political gatherings producing genuinely public spaces through the appearance, and return, of the people: the end of the end of history. These struggles have shown that people matter both through their demand for new social rights (right to decent housing, a safe environment, stable income) and by their capacity to generate material supports that enable such demands to be nourished. As the *indignados* declared: '[t]he struggle for our rights as human beings underlies everything we have demanded in every square and every demonstration in this historic year of global change.'

While the heat of these struggles has subsided in many places (with the inevitable criticism of incoherence and political ignorance from those on the left and the right) their continuing significance lies in their refusal to adapt their expressions of anger to the all too familiar media-politics of sound-bite and latest trend. While they refuse the crisis ('We will not pay for your crisis') and existing forms of representative democracy ('They don't represent us') they do not, and cannot, have a clear alternative already formed. There is no returning to the 'security' of the 'real' economy (pre-finance), or the patronage of a dominant state (social democratic). History is at a turning point in this respect. The movements of refusal and creation are pushing beyond the horizon of the possible and in so doing constituting forms of democratic and material participation that are characterized by their openness to experiment and their respect for each who takes part.

The actual being present at assemblies, forums and meetings brings together the political and the material, the opportunity to speak and the need to eat. This is a living pre-figurative politics rather than the ossified representational politics of old. Through this form of participation the subject is constituted through the process of taking part. The importance of this living-ness, of participation as process, is encapsulated by the decision made by the Madrid Puerta del Sol Commission for International Outreach on December 19th, 2011. After an assembly discussion the group decided to suspend its activity and declare itself on indefinite active reflection:

The public space we had rediscovered has been replaced once again by a sum of private spaces... The success of the movement depends on us being the 99% once again. Although we do not have the answer to what has to come next, what shape the restart we need can take, we understand that the first step for escaping from the wrong dynamic is to break with it: to stop, hold back, and get perspective.

This modesty reflects a recognition that politics is a process of individual and collective transformation not an urgent rushing forth dictated by the temporality of the crisis. Such transformations do not begin from any prior position or claim but from an openness; a beginning not an end.

Nor is this openness for openness' sake (a criticism often directed at the new forms of politics). The ruins from which alternatives must be fashioned are not only the ruins of a destructive capitalist economy but equally, or more so, the ruins of traditional forms of politics. The ideas, metaphors, categories and identities inherited from this past saturate our imaginations and actions. Accepting that there is no historical subject waiting in the wings, no agent who we can look to, requires recognizing that we are the ones we have been waiting for. The importance of openness lies in creating spaces and times outside the dominant architecture and temporality of the past and present in order to create new alliances and subjectivities based on a common dignity. These forms of politics must be able to find the space and time for all people, producing new forms of commonality which are not based on nationality, occupation, ethnicity, intellectual capacity or any of the other identities which drive us apart. This form of participation springs not from pre-existing ideas or forms of organization but from the immediate and naked recognition of ourselves together.

I lost my land, a single tractor took my land. I am alone and I am bewildered. And in the night one family camps in a ditch and another family pulls in and the tents come out. The two men squat on their hams and the women and children listen. Here is the node, you who hate change and fear revolution. Keep these two squatting men apart; make them hate, fear, suspect each other. Here is the anlage of the thing you fear. This is the zygote. For here "I lost my land" is changed; a cell is split and from its splitting grows the thing you hate - "We lost our land." The danger is here, for two men are not as lonely and perplexed as one.[2]

---

[1] Steinbeck, J. (2000). *The Grapes of Wrath*. London: Penguin, pp.35-36.
[2] Steinbeck, *The Grapes of Wrath*, p.157.

'Barriers' to Participation and Capitalist Temporalities

Patrick Bresnihan (P.B.) and Leila Dawney (L.D.)

P.B. The statement, 'we have no time to participate', communicates two common understandings. The first is that there is or could be a 'proper' time to participate. This says more about what people consider participation to be than it does about time management. Participation in this sense is understood to be a formal activity separated from daily life. Perhaps attending a community stakeholder meeting or taking part in a protest or signing a petition. Participation is stripped from the fabric of everyday life and turned into a specific exercise for those who decide they want to 'make a difference'. While this is important it is also true that what goes by the name of 'participation' today is little more than the voicing of opinions. The recognition of this adds to the growing sense of cynicism we feel about the world: the thought that 'participation' does little or nothing to change the conditions under which we live our lives. The obvious example here is the 'democratic' election every four years where we are given the opportunity to choose our government. Even this brief moment of 'participation' is spurned by more and more people, not because they 'don't have time' but because people are (rightly in most cases) disillusioned with existing forms of representative politics.

The second common understanding is that our time is already accounted for and that this is somehow inescapable: there is no time to do anything other than what we are already doing. This seems apparent when the immediate pressures of getting on with our lives (paying rent, child minders, education, health care and mounting debts) means that most of our time is spent working to make wages that never seem enough.

But the sense that we don't have any time refers to something more specific about the temporalities of contemporary capitalism. Stable jobs and fixed incomes are no longer the norm for workers today. This is not necessarily a bad thing – there is a reason why people struggled against the boredom and drudgery of factory work. However, rather than granting us more time and autonomy, the re-formation of capitalist production over the past forty years has meant that now we never seem to stop working! The social, technical and material developments that have determined this situation are complex. Three defining elements of contemporary work life can be identified here. First, the shift from industrial production to immaterial production has placed a premium on our intellectual, social, creative and affective activity, activity which does not obey the temporal limits of 0900-1700, or the spatial limits of the office. Second, the development and generalized use of new media technology has meant we are (must be) connected at all times. Thirdly, the liberalization and globalization of the labour market has meant the proliferation of flexible, short term employment contracts. For those lucky enough to have paid employment the chances are this won't last long, meaning the task of looking ahead for the next opportunity is never over.

These three elements combine in the figure of the precarious worker. Moving in and out of work, education and various forms of social welfare, the precarious worker is always having to orientate him or herself to the rapidly changing demands of the labour market. This requires being well-networked in order to respond quickest to opportunities. As public provision in the form of social welfare, health, education and housing is cut back, more and more of the population are being subjected to this condition. In the UK and Ireland precarity has been institutionalised through the welfare system: if recipients do not show they are working to get work they cannot be assured of payments in the future. The lesson is clear: if we are not improving ourselves through more education or training; if we are not 'putting ourselves out there' in order to network; if we are not applying for more jobs, for more funding, grants and contracts, then we are not doing enough. This knowledge - that our time is not even money but the faint hope of money in the future - demands that we subordinate more and more of our days and nights to self-improvement. We internalise this future-orientated time;

it envelops our waking life and spills into our anxious dreams about what tomorrow might bring.

L.D. *The condition of always having to be switched on not only collapses distinctions between 'work' and 'leisure', it also imposes a frenetic and fragmented rhythm to our daily lives. So, while we share this condition with our fellow nomads we rarely, if ever, share any length of time with them. We do not clock on and clock off at the same time. At best we meet each other in fleeting encounters; brief moments in which to tell each other we don't have the time to talk. The need to work on ourselves, preparing for whatever opportunity may arise, is perhaps the most insidious way in which we become individualised. We find ourselves wanting to engage in mutual or common projects, of being involved in a meaningful way, but the constantly shifting landscape of the future undermines these attempts, breaking our present commitments by opening up new opportunities which we 'must' take.*

These pressures on our time mean is that there is very little left to do anything 'more', including getting involved in our communities, in decision making, in trying to make a change. In much writing about participation, barriers to participation are identified that might include a lack of engagement, apathy, disenfranchisement or individualism, barriers that can be 'lifted' through working with specific community groups to encourage them to engage more, through for example a community arts project or a citizen's participation project such as a citizens' jury. This idea that projects such as these can get people more involved in public life, however, simply compounds the idea that a lack of engagement with public life is our fault. It places of the problem of a perceived crisis in participation at the hands of individuals and groups, instead of considering the structural nature of barriers to participation.

If we want people to get more involved with the world outside their own immediate, pressing and material concerns, we need to turn this thinking on its head and consider the temporal and spatial structuring of social life that leads to a lack of time and space for participation. So, instead of asking why people do not participate as much as they might, we need to consider what determining forces structure their social, economic, affective and experiential lives such that participation is neither possible nor desirable. We also need to move away from the assumption that participation in political decision making is a possible and desirable move for everybody if those barriers are removed.

As we have seen, there is little time for other activities when one works a 40 hour week, and maintains a home and family at the same time. When this amount of time spent working is necessary both for having a job to begin with (the "normal working week") and for paying housing and living costs. When one's commitments to caring for family members, or for self-improvement preclude the time and the will for active participation: when one is expected to maintain one's appearance, to cook and eat healthy and fresh meals, and to conform to the many expectations that saturate our time. These pressures on time are by and large the effects of the market, and need to be considered as such, rather than as a lack of engagement by individuals. The colonising and saturating instinct of market forces produces anxieties, desires, needs, all the while incorporating more and more of our activity and labours into its charge. Housing and energy costs, and the structure of the normal working week, mean that it is unrealistic to expect most economically active people to participate in public life in a formal manner, or to move their activities outwards and act for change. Decisions are made about people's lives by professional politicians, and people feel too fatigued and detached from political processes to do anything about them. This separation of politics and productive life, then, is a function of the relationship between state, market and society. Identifying these problems as being problems of the market, problems in the way in which resources are distributed and allocated, rather than an individual problem, leads to a number of ways in which these problems can be addressed or overcome.

We need to consider how to rethink these distributions and allocations in order to enable space and time for participation. The temporalities and spatialities of life in late capitalist society do not at present enable this to happen. This could be changed by a radical restructuring of the way in which the economy is organized through labour time, for example through a shorter working week, through workplace based participation, through a redistribution of employment, or through capping of housing costs. These are structural solutions that respond to a structural problem: They move the point of focus from the individual to the way in which time and resource allocation produce ways of life that are at present incompatible with participating in a shared world. By moving and redistributing labour time and resources, we would all have more time to participate.

P.B. But there is something depressing about accepting that our lives are already entirely colonised by contemporary capitalism. We give up something when we agree with the statement: 'we don't have the time'. We give up something *and* we grant power to capitalism. We accept that we have none of our own time because capitalist time saturates every aspect of our lives. We accept that it is not just our working lives which are subject to the logic of capitalist command and discipline but the way we value our activities in the present and orientate ourselves to the future. We find ourselves trapped in a cage with our only strategy for change being an analysis of its structures and a faint hope that we can reform them. But where is the political subject capable of effecting even the smallest change to this situation? And why should we accept that capitalism already owns our time?

There are fault-lines which run across our everyday lives. These fault-lines refuse the idea, made by capitalists and their critics, that we are all already incorporated into the heart of capitalist life. We are not entirely determined by limited job prospects in the future, or the measures and criteria which decide if we are being productive or not. We break with these insidious forms of instrumentalism every time we do something for no reason, when we slow down in order to attend to those around us, or allow ourselves to be interrupted by a different concern, one perhaps that shouldn't be ours. These moments can be as ordinary as spending an afternoon with a friend when you should be working, or forgetting the pressures of an assignment or the thought of the alarm clock through the rich time being spent with people in the present. These are moments when we love or care for something outside of its role or function within an assumed economy of meaning and value. Of course these moments are transient and ephemeral and can not in themselves replace capitalism. But they are moments of excess which shift our attention away from the structures of capitalist domination towards the many, everyday ways in which people already escape into different rhythms and social relations.

Through his re-telling of the story of Robinson Crusoe, Alain Tournier shows us how the sudden fracturing of time can open up previously unimaginable events and relations.[1] At first the story begins very much like Daniel Defoe's original. Finding himself alone Robinson is terrified that he will fall into an animal-like state if he doesn't attempt to construct and maintain all the structures of the civilization he has left behind. He throws himself into work, colonizing and taming more and more areas of the island. While he satisfies some needs he does not escape the constant fear that his work is not enough. He has fear that he will run out of food, that the rodents will eat his grain, that he will wake one day and not know himself anymore.

In an effort to control this fear of the future he creates a way of measuring time with some bamboo and a supply of water. He counts the hours, and marks the passing days on a wooden calendar, allowing him to monitor his progress and plan ahead. It is not just Robinson that is taken in by this ordering of time but all the life he has brought within his command: now there is a time for sowing, planting, watering; a time for waking and sleeping; a time for rest on the Sabbath. His interactions with the island become dominated by these routines, as well as the constant worry that he has not utilised his time sufficiently, that something more could be done.

One day Robinson forgets to fill the water clock. On waking he notices immediately that the sound of the water has stopped. His first reaction is horror, and then relief. He stretches in his bunk and realises that he doesn't need to perform his chores that morning. He thinks to himself that without time passing the life of the island must be on hold. So he wanders around the island, exploring hollows and caves he had not previously brought himself to visit. He notices colorful birds high up in the branches and the sounds of the jungle became discernible as more than a throbbing backdrop. He moves in directions which he does not decide, carried by nothing more than a new and radiant openness to the island. For the first time Robinson glimpses *another island* behind the one he had been trying to control. This island flowers and flourishes for its own sake, a fact which had been hidden behind his own daily preoccupations. Here we see how the apparent reality of organized, instrumental time can break down, liberating new relations and possibilities.

L.D. *To think the world differently, to make a break with the idea that our lives are colonised by capitalism is all very well, but there are nevertheless real, material, objective forces that act upon us and constrain our power to act differently. There are people who rely on us to feed and clothe and house us; there* *are expectations of decent social being that we feel obliged to make. To simply decide not to buy into these temporalities is not an option for most of us. Structures do act on us, and constrain us in very real, material ways.*

So any movement to contest this saturation of our time, to live in these fault lines, has to take place within the context of our material needs. Not just our basic needs, but our needs to live in a society that invariably does make demands of us, that we cannot just refuse to buy into without radical changes to our lives. Given the perceived impossibility of these structural changes impacting on our lives any time soon, there are real, material things we can do, in terms of the local distribution and allocation of time and resources, which can help us to participate more. This involves thinking about making space for participation through collectivisation. We may consider how to enable those whose current economic position already leaves them open to more active participation: those who are currently outside of work regimes and lack the opportunities to participate. For example those engaged in caring for young children could create collectivised childcare arrangements that enable those spaces to be not only spaces of care but spaces of active participation in social and political life. In this way, playgroups become learning and community action centres. Children at school are also outside of the wage economy and could be encouraged to become involved in making social worlds. Village meals (in France, the 'repas de commune', or 'repas populaire') take the burden of cooking away from each household for one day a week, and provide a space to think, to talk, dance, share food and exchange ideas. Schools could also be spaces of participation. Retired people, who may also be carers, are in a position to participate too, if collective spatial and temporal solutions are devised to take care of other needs and responsibilities, freeing their time for participation.

But this is not about ensuring that everyone is productive, or putting people to work. This is not a call for a punitive system that forces the economically inactive into capitalist temporalities of self-improvement and job-seeking. This is about enabling those who are in a position to engage in fulfilling, collective ways of being and living to take advantage of the luxury of their time – to be involved in something which is actively concerned with creating a better – and easier – world, and producing non capitalist spaces where there is time – time to talk, to think, to work together. It is about seeing where the fault lines are and taking them for our collective selves. These fault lines are not just about refusing to participate in neoliberal temporalities. They are about providing material alternatives to the structures and spaces of everyday life that take away our time, and free us to spend time not being productive within capitalism, but acting and making worlds outside of these temporalities that in doing so, changes those temporalities.

P.B. As Karl Marx pointed out many years ago, the ways in which we organise our material resources do other things too – they have an effect on our consciousness. By doing things differently; by acting as though we could make things easier by working together rather than separately, we can do more than just change what we do: we can change how we think, experience and understand the world.

Of course it is not enough to think ourselves beyond capitalism, as though its hold was mere illusion or ideology a dream. It is precisely the need to attend to concrete experience and the way in which it materialises through and between people and things that provides us with a point from which to create different worlds.

The structuring of contemporary capitalism imposes new constraints on our lives. The scarcity of employment opportunities and the frenetic speed of global capital demands that we work harder than ever for even less reward. This is real, and many people experience its violence every day. But our experiences are not reducible to this violence and exploitation. We are not just bodies in reserve, human capital, expendable. The fault lines are the many instances, hardly perceptible, where people combine to produce different forms of common life at a distance from capitalist valorisation and discipline.

The question is how to attend to and expand these combinations. It is certainly not enough to romanticise them, downplaying the power of capital to close them down or co-opt the value they create. It is also true that we live in depoliticised times when the thought of a world beyond capitalism and representative, parliamentary democracy are still considered extreme and inappropriate. In such a context any hope of developing a collective process of participation must engage with what does exist: the nascent, uncertain and ambiguous frustrations and joys which motivate people to act and come together. These are the fault-lines which are becoming more visible since the economic collapse. But they are not just cries of desperation. Into the vacuum of politics they are whispers of the return of history, of something else maybe being possible, dim as it may seem.

Recognizing the importance of thinking and feeling differently does not mean ignoring the significance of material resources (production and distribution) for individual and collective activity. Creating different temporalities in which different subjectivities can experiment and develop requires material supports and resources. The coming together of people and their capacities (to cook, build, make, share, socialise) and materials (buildings, technologies, food, spaces) produces a kind of commons which allows people, even temporarily, to escape the self-exploitation and fragmentation that characterises so many other aspects of our lives. Coming together and finding ways of supporting ourselves collectively makes it possible, in small ways, to breathe a sigh of relief, to do things in a time and space which are free from the logic of productivity.

As a first step, this coming together is not based on any common identity or political strategy but a more pragmatic and immediate desire to escape the competition and pressure we experience as precarious workers. Put simply, coming together like this can make it possible to live more and work less because doing things collectively is the only way we can be free from the obligation to work so hard as self-exploiting individuals. This is not primarily a question of politics or protest. It is more a question of fostering ways of escaping immediately and materially the pressures we experience today within contemporary capitalism. In these times and spaces our atomised hurtling onwards is stilled and the people and things we are engaging with appear as something else, as things which cannot be skipped over.

---

[1] Tournier, M. (1974) *Friday, or the Other Island*, trans. N. Denny. London: Penguin.

Commodification and ‘the Commons’

Samuel Kirwan

One reason a greater level of participation seems so important, and yet so difficult to achieve, is that so many of the spaces through which we move seem designed to isolate us – to isolate us from other people, from new experiences or from unwanted emotions. The concept of ‘commodification’, describing the reconfiguration of experience into measurable flows that allow life to be directed towards productive and profitable goals, can help us understand this dynamic. While our attention is constantly being captured by our surroundings, it is only to direct us on experiential trajectories aligned not to communication and cooperation but to the isolating practices of consumption.

One outcome of this commodification of space is fear; a fear of the marginalised, of the young, of ambiguous spaces and unexpected experiences. Too often the promotion of 'participation' is ready to play to this fear, celebrating the creation of closed spaces in which the range of practices is firmly demarcated. In contrast, this book seeks to speak for a space that opens experiences, that abandons the closely held feeling of communal *unity*. It is useful, in this context, to return to the language of 'the commons' – the term carried from the pre-enclosed spaces that harboured shared traditions and practices shared between generations. To mobilise this term is not to harbour a nostalgic longing for a prelapsarian golden age, but rather to create the commons in our own small ways; creating spaces that connect across boundaries, that respond to our fears with creativity and openness. To participate, in this context, is not only to act communally (this assumption has undermined the field of participatory projects) – it is to allow for the broadening of horizons in this engagement of the commons.

To give an example of such an opening, we may turn to public parks. Urban green spaces are often seen as the antithesis of the commons, inasmuch as many were created in the Victorian era, towards the end of the rapid enclosures of the industrial era, as an attempt to reform the unruly and immoral practices of the working class. Urban parks, it is argued, were attempts to shape the morals of the working rabble through the orderly and pristine shaping of space.[1] Yet they are often the space in which this ordering is broken down. Historians have also noted how shared practices emerged from illicit re-appropriations of park spaces, and in the present we may note how events such as communal drawing projects (in which materials are left for the painting of paths and walkways) enact a momentary breaking down of who is able to shape the park space.[2] In other words, parks may be seen as 'commons', and as such as spaces of participation, inasmuch as they provide a platform for experiences that transgress the divisions established by the commodification of space.

---

[1] Taylor, A. (1995). ""Commons Stealers"," Land-Grabbers" and" Jerry Builders": Space, Popular Radicalism and the Politics of Public Access in London, 1848-1880." *International Review of Social History*, 40: 383-408.

[2] Bailey, P. (1987). *Leisure and Class in Victorian England: Rational Recreation and the Contest for Control, 1830-1885*. London: Routledge & Kegan Paul. p.186

Making Common Worlds

An Ethos For Participation

Leila Dawney

Feeling part of something.

One way of thinking about participation is through paying attention to those things that we do that help to build worlds together, and in doing so, interrupt the story that society is made up of individuals and families and governments, with nothing in between. In other words, the common story that is told about the way in which we participate in society is through our relationship to our immediate families, and through our relationship to the State (what it does for us/what we have to give it) as individuals and families. The ethos for participation that I outline here stems from the idea that it is OK to think that we know better than others, and to act on that; and the idea of looking beyond our immediate worlds and thinking about the knock-on effects. I would like us to tell stories about how we make common worlds. If we *feel* like we are in common – that we have shared stakes that extend beyond the immediate, yet are not based on a contractual arrangement with a State that we see as providing services for us as individuals – then we can foster an ethos of collective responsibility and care towards the world. We can produce the social.

This can lead us to think about how the *feeling of being in common* is produced in different spaces and through different practices. These practices might include overtly political attempts to redefine the 'commons', or to reclaim particular spaces as held in common (for example the occupy movement), as well as those practices that also contribute to a sense of shared experience – that produce conviviality (common life), like eating, undergoing trauma, or parenthood. So instead of thinking about the common in terms of a political position, identity or movement, the common becomes these diverse sites of practice.

Analysing these sites helps us to think about how a sense of being in common, a sense of making a shared world, is achieved; what situations resonate and 'grip' us. Politics works when they are felt, when they resonate with lived experience. If they are felt bodily, they have weight: they carry. And this means that our experience of living in the world allows for some ideas to stick and for some to not. So some claims to solidarity, such as those of occupy, I argue, may alienate many people, because there is a disconnect, a disjuncture ... *'you say we are the 99%, but I am not like you, or you'...*

So it is important to think about how and why some movements, and some rhetorical devices, have "grip" while others do not, and who they grip, and who they might alienate. Claims to be in-common are augmented affectively through lived experience and struggle. For example, the daily experience of labour as necessity or obligation is resonant with the production and augmentation of a sense of an "us" as hard-working, tax-paying citizens. Press images of protestors who do not work, and whose upper-middle class background is stressed do not resonate with the experience of most working- and middle-class lives. Their authority to speak on behalf of others is undermined by their distance from the lived experience of those others, and the constant accentuation of that difference in the media.

So if we are to think about how to make people feel part of something, to feel like they have collective stakes, it is important to consider the material ways in which the common is produced that organises bodies so that a sense of shared life is enabled and fostered. This can take place through the ordering of spaces – low fences and back alleys were highlighted in the sociologist Valerie Walkerdine's discussion of how working class communities in a Steelworks Town felt in common – and through objects (community defibrillators, memorials, tea, PCs) as well as through the things that people say and do.[1] One approach to this is to draw attention to specific moments through which a sense of the common is produced – moments that may be unexpected – and then look at what is going on in that moment. These moments are sites of the political and may indeed take place in 'unframed' spaces, for example in moments of shared dwelling that give rise to a conviviality that exceeds the political framing of an event of occupation.

Walkerdine discusses communal 'beingness' as a sense of holding or containment (being held). She writes of this containment as being produced in the Steelworks Town, through "a long history of difficult and dangerous work, which must produce an anxiety about annihilation and the necessity to find ways of coping which could produce a sense of the continuity and security to counter the extreme uncertainty of the employment situation".[2] So a sense of shared being, the production of common life, emerges in this instance as a way of coping with material conditions of precarity and struggle. It is not invoked; rather it takes place as a result of material and affective conditions of shared existence.

A politics of the common

If lived experience can lead to this sense of being and becoming part of something, of partaking in a common world, then we can think about what can be done to bring this about – to cast the net wider. In other words, we can consider how "practices of the common" can be used as a counter strategy to regimes of individualisation. We can think about how to nurture these collective ways of being, in order to produce a sense of the "we" that is keenly felt.

Through conversations with a range of practitioners of participatory democracy I have started to think about this idea of having shared stakes and how these collective stakes can move us to do things that extend beyond our immediate mode of concern. And this is also about moving away from the family/state dichotomy that I mentioned at the beginning, which neoliberal individualism and big state policies lead to. It involves, instead, thinking about shared spaces that can be claimed as collective. This claiming renames the stakes as common, and means that we are participating in making the world beyond our immediate desires and needs.

I have also started to think about the collective power of small acts: we are social creatures, and we learn from each other. It is only when we see others doing something that we think it's OK to do it ourselves. In the spirit of this, as an experiment in making common worlds, I have started to pick up litter when I'm walking along, to weed and sweep the pavement and road near my house, and to look after the communal kitchen area at work. These small acts of commoning are important: their ethic of care fosters a mode of being in the world which engages us as active subjects. This is not "big society"; but it is a reaction to cultures of entitlement, dependency and resentment that breed inactivity and isolation.

---

[1] Walkerdine, V. (2010) 'Communal beingness and affect: an exploration of the trauma of an ex-industrial community' *Body & Society* 16(1): 91-116
[2] Walkerdine, 'Communal beingness', p.98

Participation and Gifts

Samuel Kirwan

The obligation attached to a gift itself is not inert. Even when abandoned by the giver, it still forms a part of him. Through it he has a hold over the recipient, just as he had, while its owner, a hold over anyone who stole it. For the *taonga* is animated with the *hau* of its forest, its soil, its homeland, and the *hau* pursues him who holds it.[1]

Marcel Mauss, referring here to Maori practices of exchanging gifts, where the *hau* refers to the 'spirit of things' and *taonga* to the object given, provides an ambiguous starting point when considering the central role of gift-giving to the production of identities, relationships and ultimately cultures. From the *Potlatch*, a gathering within certain native American tribes where goods were both freely distributed and destroyed, to the *kula* of Melanesia, an inter-tribal trade event defined by ritual acts of generosity, Mauss captures the *vitality* of the gift – its life *beyond* the interested parties. Yet he does so only in order to contain the gift within particular economies of gift-exchange. For although 'in theory' such gifts are given, received and reciprocated voluntarily, "they are in essence strictly obligatory, and their sanction is private or open warfare." [2] Mauss's project was to uncover the economies of exchange that shaped these obligations to give, receive and reciprocate. The gift, in other words, could be explained as an alternative form of economy, its giving as an interest-oriented action "the motives of such excessive gifts and reckless consumption, such mad losses and destruction of wealth", lay ultimately in the self-interest of the giver or destroyer.

Mauss nonetheless raises some fascinating aspects of gift-giving. What characterises the gift, as opposed to a present, is its uniqueness – the level of personal labour or effort embodied in it. Gifts are profoundly personal:"one gives away what is in reality a part of one's nature and substance, while to receive something is to receive a part of someone's spiritual essence." The giving of a gift, in other words, is more than the simple exchange of objects with monetary value, one is relinquishing part of oneself and thereby forming an enduring bond with another. Again, however, Mauss seeks to contain this within a strict economy of self-interest, noting that it is this very investment of personality in an object that makes it dangerous for the receiver not to reciprocate. As David Graeber argues, despite seeking to explore alternative economic systems, Mauss belongs to a long tradition of seeing 'the logic of the marketplace' lurking beneath diverse cultural practices. [3]

There is, however, another perspective on the gift in its vitality and uniqueness, one that would concentrate not on the containment of the gift within a system of exchange, but conversely on the *excess* of the gift, the refusal that it should be reciprocated in kind, or moreover that the kinds of bonds the gift creates, such as those between parents and children, cannot be defined by rational self-interest. This is derived from Mauss's contemporary, Georges Bataille[4], for whom it was the *irrational* aspect of the gift that deserves our attention – its capacity to *disrupt* any such uniform system. Theodor Adorno notes the decline of gift-giving in this *excessive* sense in the, now well established, principle of the exchangeable present, "which signifies to the recipient: take this, it's all yours, do what you like with it; if you don't want it, that's all the same to me, get something else instead."[5]

The difference between these two perspectives on the gift is, I think, informative for our considerations of participation. On the one hand one may see participation as the repayment of a debt; the return on all the benefits the community, state or particular institution have afforded the individual over their life. We participate in something external to us, returning to our proper lives when this debt is repaid. On the other participation is something personal, unique and excessive. To say that the gift is not inert is to recognise that it *breaks out* of the system of exchange: the value thus produced in such acts is not measurable with reference to debts accrued elsewhere, but is a *value in itself*. The statement that the gift bears a personal element, rather than a recognition of the duty to reciprocate, is a recognition the extent to which we are personally invested, and personally transformed, in the labours of kindness and generosity that constitute participation. In sum, participation is less an act of duty than one of love.

It is clear, however, that the former perspective dominates discussion of participation, circulating around means of forcing people to recognise their civic duty, and it is worth placing this in the wider expansion of indebtedness as a cultural condition. David Graeber argues that the interplay between debt and love was at the heart of the socio-economic system of endless credit and consumption, and as such upon the deepening indebtedness of those who dared to live beyond the parameters of mere survival. If people continued, stubbornly, in their "insistence on continuing to love one another",[6] sharing their houses with relatives and their alcohol with friends, the tendency to replace financial supports with proliferating means of credit responded by "continually converting love into debt".[7] As debt became ubiquitous, Graeber notes the emergence of a new moral doctrine of debt repayment, one used to stigmatise the poor and also to urge them into more productive acts in 'the community'.

In the United Kingdom, this latter tendency, reaching its nadir with the concept of 'The Big Society', can be seen in the extent to which 'participation', whether in the affairs of the community, the city or the nation, has come to be considered a *responsibility* of citizens. This sentiment was most clearly expressed in a key phrase adopted by 'New Labour', one chosen to express its drive to make the services provided by the state conditional upon one's participation in civic life: "no rights without responsibilities". Citizens were posed as being originarily in debt to the state, their participation being less an act of generosity than the reciprocation of accumulated favours.

The poverty of this approach is made clear by any attempt to draw equivalences between services and participative acts; could way say, for example, that a day of education enjoyed by one's children, might be worth two hours of repairing the benches in a local park? That unemployment benefits should be conditional upon voluntary activity in the community?[8] It is an approach that severs individuals and acts from their contexts; we are no longer people, with interests, cares, loves and anxieties, but interchangeable agents within a general system of exchange. Acts of kindness, generosity and love become reduced, as in Mauss's study, to the reciprocating of favours, always 'given and repaid under obligation'.

The new ethos of participation we are setting out in this book retains the notion that participation is a gift given under no obligation, and that its product is a *value in itself*. This entails a re-formulation of the questions upon which the participative field is based. Rather than asking how individuals can be made to recognise their civic duty, we might ask how individuals, considered in the context of their work and care commitments, can be better supported in their existing practices of participation. Rather than asking how participation can better 'fill-in' for existing services, we might ask how participation can enrich and transform individual personalities. Rather than asking, under the rubric of regeneration, how participation can ensure local economic growth, we might ask how it might create enduring spaces for continuing the long history of gift-giving.

[1] Mauss, M. (1966) *The Gift: Forms and Functions of Exchange in Archaic Societies*, London: Cohen and West, p.9

[2] Mauss, *The Gift*, p.3

[3] Graeber, D. (2011) *Debt: The First 5,000 Years*, New York: Melville House.

[4] Bataille, G. (1949) *La Part Maudite*, Paris: Minuit.

[5]Adorno, T. (2005) [1951], *Minima Moralia: Reflections on a Damaged Life*, London: Verso, p. 42.

[6] Graeber, *Debt*, p. 379.

[7] Graeber, *Debt* p. 386.

[8] The latter is currently enforced under the Mandatory Work Activity Scheme. Department for Work and Pensions (DWP), (2012), Mandatory Work Activity Scheme Extended available from: http://www.dwp.gov.uk/newsroom/press-releases/2012/jun-2012/dwp061-12.shtml, accessed 16/11/12.

Postscript

How did this book come about? A diverse group of academics interested in various aspects of 'participation' were brought together through the UK Arts and Humanities Research Council's (AHRC) 'Connected Communities' programme. The group included practitioners of participatory democracy, participatory theatre, critical pedagogy and research on politics, power and authority. The main organizers were a longstanding collaborative group, the Authority Research Network (ARN). For one week in the summer of 2012, the ARN organized a week-long 'collaborative thinking' retreat for the eleven participants. In preparation for the retreat, we held consultations with two participatory activist groups, the Stepping Out Theatre Company, and the Mad Hatters of Bath. We also produced a literature survey of participation, compiled a set of key readings, and carried out and wrote up interviews with all the participants.

At the retreat we were able to hold focused discussion sessions around the key readings, ideas and examples of participation, separated from the hubbub of our everyday lives. We limited the range of materials we had access to, organized activities in rolling pairs, and combined intensive work sessions with cooking, cleaning, walking and eating. Over the week, we were able to discuss problems of participation in a spirit of friendship and the context of a long-term commitment to collaborative thinking, openly sharing and drawing upon one another's experiences, perspectives and reflections. The conversations sometimes took time to get going, taking place within safe spaces that we constructed during the week. One of our challenges was to ensure that conflict and disagreement were not stifled, but facilitated, by the safety of the spaces.

We developed a certain craft of 'conversation management'. We experimented with our conversations about participation along several dimensions – speeding up and slowing down discussions, rearranging groups and pairings, altering the heterogeneity of the space of discussion and adjusting the intensity of our engagement with one other. We saw how the best insights often came when *not* focusing on the problems at hand (though often primed by focused discussions). We found ways of luring agreements, disagreements, near-consensuses, total disagreements and productive alliances.

We remain divided as to how 'participatory' our event was. It was not a participatory event in many conventional senses of the term: it was deliberately exclusive and very time-demanding. However, much like a 'consensus conference', it was productive in bringing very different viewpoints together and into constructive dialogue. Despite the values associated with participation, perhaps even because those values are so important and widespread, we would argue that it is important to periodically make the time and space to benefit from the virtues of critical distance. Whilst the event was not participatory it certainly was highly *collaborative*. Perhaps it is the case that real collaboration places transitory limits upon participation; indeed, the difference between 'collaboration' and 'participation' is itself an excellent problem, ripe for further exploration and conversation!

The project, funded by a grant from the AHRC Connected Communities programme, was called "Authority, Knowledge and Performance in Participatory Practice". The grant paid for accommodation at, and travel to, the retreat, as well as salaries for the time spent by researchers carrying out preparatory work and writing up results, and consultation fees for Stepping Out Theatre Company and Mad Hatters of Bath. In addition to this collection of essays, the researchers have produced a website, including reviews of the exiting literature on participation that will be particularly interesting to students and researchers (www.authorityresearch.net/participatory-practice.html), and an academic article which sets out an extended report and discussion of conclusions from the project.

Finally, a special thanks to Erin Walcon, who was the 11th participant on the retreat, but was unable to contribute an article to this collection.

About the Authors

Claire Blencowe lectures in Sociology at Warwick University. She has led collaborative projects including 'Immanent Authority and the Making of Community' and 'Authority, Knowledge and Performance in Participatory Practice'. Publications include *Biopolitical Experience: Foucault, Power & Positive Critique* (Palgrave, 2012) and articles in *Theory Culture & Society* and *History of the Human Sciences.*

Contact : C.Blencowe@warwick.ac.uk

Patrick Bresnihan is a researcher based in Dublin. His research examines the dynamics of enclosure and the politics of the common in various historical and contemporary contexts. His PhD analysed governmental responses to the problem of overfishing and the way these responses function to police a finite world (nature) within global capitalism. He is part of an autonomous research and education collective called The Provisional University.

Contact: bresnip@tcd.ie

Julian Brigstocke lectures in human geography at Plymouth University. His research focuses on contemporary political theory, urban avant-gardes, contemporary architectures of authority, and the politics of aesthetics. His book *The Life of the City: Space, Humour and the Authority of Experience in Late Nineteenth Century Montmartre* will be published with Ashgate in 2013.

Contact: Julian.Brigstocke@plymouth.ac.uk

Leila Dawney is a Lecturer in Human Geography at the University of Brighton, UK. Her research interests include cultural geographies of embodied practice, performance and landscape, Spinoza and new materialist theory, new authority studies and neoliberal subjectivities.

Contact: L.Dawney@brighton.ac.uk

Samuel Kirwan is a Research Officer at the Office for National Statistics, holding research interests in the theory, practice and policy of community. He is currently editing a book on the subject of 'the commons'.

Contact: kirwan.samuel@gmail.com

Naomi Millner is a political and economic geographer, with a background in migration issues, the study of social movements, and the geographies of new political formations. She is interested in applying cultural and political theory to understand changing relations of power and knowledge in a globalising context. She is currently a Lecturer in Human Geography at the University of Bristol, as well as working as a volunteer in refugee organisations and popular education initiatives.

Contact: naomimillner@googlemail.com

Helen Nicholson is professor of theatre and performance at Royal Holloway, University of London, where she specialises in applied theatre. She is currently leading two research projects, one on the contribution the arts make to the culture of dementia care, and the other is a major new research project on amateur dramatics.

Contact: H.Nicholson@rhul.ac.uk

Tehseen Noorani is based in Washington DC, where he divides his time between academic research, community development and activism. He is working on a scoping study for the University of Bristol and Cardiff University on how the term 'co-production' is mobilised in participatory research. His research has focused on mental healthcare, exploring the connections between wellness and political capacity. He has worked with grassroots self-help networks and community advocacy forums in both the UK and the USA.

Contact: tehs.noorani@googlemail.com

Jenny Pearce is Professor of Latin American Politics and Director of the International Centre for Participation Studies in the Department of Peace Studies, University of Bradford. She is a specialist in issues of violence, conflict, social change and social agency in Latin America and has published widely on these themes. More recently she has also worked on problems of participation and conflict in the north of England.

Contact: j.v.pearce@bradford.ac.uk

Tom Wakeford is Senior Research Fellow and course leader of Community Participation in Professional Practice at the University of Edinburgh. He uses action research approaches to contribute to emerging self-critical movements for social and environmental justice. His recent projects have sought to craft new means of dialogue and mutual learning between those people whose perspectives have been marginalised in the past and others working at institutions that have traditionally been seen as centres of expertise.

Contact: wakeford.tom@gmail.com